Birdflight

As The Basis Of

Aviation

Compiled from the Results of Numerous Experiments made
By O. and G. Lilienthal

WITH A BIOGRAPHICAL INTRODUCTION AND
ADDENDUM
BY
GUSTAV LILIENTHAL
ARCHITECT AND TEACHER AT THE HUMBOLDT ACADEMY

*TRANSLATED FROM THE SECOND EDITION
BY
A.W. ISENTHAL, A.M.I.E.E., F.R.P.S.*

1 PORTRAIT, 94 ILLUSTRATIONS, AND 8 LITHO. PLATES

A Contribution
Towards a System
of Aviation

Otto Lilienthal

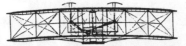

American Aeronautical Archives

Foreword and cover copyright © 2001 by Michael A. Markowski
All rights reserved under PanAmerican and
Int'l Copyright Conventions

Published by Markowski International Publishers,
One Oakglade Circle, Hummelstown, PA 17036 USA
Phone: (717)566-0468 • Fax: (717)566-6423
e-mail: amaeroarch@aol.com
American Aeronautical Archives is an imprint
of Markowski International Publishers.

1   2   3   4   5   6   7   8   9   10

This Markowski edition, published in 2001, is an unabridged
facsimile of the original work, first published in 1889 and written
by Otto Lilienthal. It includes all the original photos and illustrations.
The Preface was written in 1911 by A.W. Isenthal, the translator.
The Foreword to the Markowski Edition was specially
prepared for this edition.

Publisher's Cataloging-in-Publication
(Provided by Quality Books, Inc.)
Lilienthal, Otto, 1848-1896
    Birdflight as the Basis of Aviation: a contribution towards a
system of aviation/Otto Lilienthal; with a biographical
introduction and addendum by Gustav Lilienthal; translated
from the second edition by A.W. Isenthal. – 1st ed. p. cm.
    "Compiled from the results of numerous experiments made
by O. And G. Lilienthal."
    Includes index.
    LCCN: 99-74074
    ISBN: 0-938716-58-1

1.   Flight.   2. Birds—Flight.   3. Wings.
4.   Aerodynamics.   5. Aeronautics.
I.   Lilienthal, Gustav, 1849-1933.   II. Title.

TL570.L55 2000   629.132
                        QBI00-280

Manufactured in the United States of America

Foreword

Ever since man looked up and saw birds soaring overhead, he envied their freedom and ease of travel—and dreamed of flying. Through the ages, countless men died in pursuit of that dream, but it was Otto Lilienthal who proved it was possible. Not enough can be said about his great pioneering work. And it is to him that we can directly trace the true beginnings of human flight.

Unlike so many other bird watchers, Lilienthal, with assistance from his brother Gustave, studied the details of how birds fly. They learned precisely what a bird does with its wings—how it alters dihedral to change stability and how it varies curvature to change lift and drag in various flight situations. As a result of those observations, they recognized the superiority of curved wing surfaces and developed a "theory of flight," forming the foundation for the science of aerodynamics. And that's what *Birdflight As The Basis of Aviation* is all about. It was read by nearly every early aviation pioneer who had a serious interest in building and flying an aircraft. Otto didn't find all the answers, but he did more than anyone else—up until the Wright Brothers, who considered Otto their hero.

It is incredible when you realize that Otto's book was first published in 1889. And it's proof positive he was one of the greatest of all aviation pioneers. Until he applied his enthusiasm and engineering skill to "the problem of human flight," most previous attempts were done on a hit-or-miss, non-scientific basis. Lilienthal was truly the first person to have deliberately and audaciously committed himself to learning the secrets of the birds, and to become accustomed to gliding through the air.

Ever since I was a boy, I've been fascinated by Otto Lilienthal and his work. When I first found a copy of the original English language edition I was awestruck—what Lilienthal had accomplished in the late nineteenth century was truly amazing. That find was back in 1972, when I visited a dingy old, out-of-the-way bookstore in Boston with my good friend Tom Peghiny. He later became a world champion hang glider pilot and ultralight aircraft manufacturer. Little did we know that one day I would republish Otto's great book.

I've been "in love" with aviation all my life and republishing this classic work is a dream come true. During the process of re-reading it in early 1999, I gained an even deeper understanding of and appreciation for what Otto accomplished. He was not only a man of great vision, but also a man of action. He knew what he wanted to do, believed he could do it, and he did it. I am more inspired than ever by his daring, determination and sense of mission.

On a more personal note, I must share with you that my educational background, like Otto's, is engineering (aeronautical), and we share the same birthdate, May 23, only I appeared 99 years later! When I first read Otto's book in 1972, I got inspired to leave my job and began manufacturing hang gliders—and it changed my life. That same year I got my private pilot's license, but flying a hang glider was always more fun. I wanted to experience flight in its purest form, the way Otto did. And believe me, there is nothing like running down a hill and lifting off in full free flight. It's truly the dream of the ages fulfilled.

I consider it an honor and a privilege to republish this historically important work. I hope you enjoy the book, understand it's significance, and appreciate what Otto accomplished. Before he died, on August 9, 1896, the day after his fatal gliding accident, he uttered these immortal words: "Sacrifices must be made." His death was tragic and untimely, but the legacy he left behind launched mankind on perhaps its most daring adventure—the development of aviation. The next time you fly high in the sky in a comfortable seat onboard a jetliner, maybe you'll think of this courageous man named Otto Lilienthal—"The Father of Gliding Flight."

Blue skies and gentle breezes,

PREFACE

TWENTY years have passed since a German Engineer, Otto Lilienthal, published a systematic account of his researches in what, at that time, seemed to be a barren field : the conditions governing mechanical flight as demonstrated by birds. Until that time, and indeed even up to a comparatively recent date, the most varied and frequently impossible speculations were ripe as to the causes which enabled birds to fly. Differences in specific gravity, special construction of the skeleton, anatomical specific properties, and the like, were invented to account for the ability of birds to sustain and alter their position in the air and in some cases even the fiat went forth that man should not attempt a feat which nature had evidently denied to him, and that he should not tempt Providence.

It was therefore essentially the merit of Lilienthal, by applying his mechanical training to the problem of birdflight, and by a series of systematic investigations, to evolve some order from chaos, and to finally reduce the great mystery to a purely mechanical or dynamical proposition which, although incomplete in many respects, yet gave tangible shape to the whole, making it possible for future workers to fill the various gaps and to rectify some of the earlier assumptions which had necessarily to be made.

That, in the light of later experiments, some of Lilienthal's coefficients and equations had to be superseded, cannot detract from his merits. Such facilities as wind tunnels and Eiffel towers, in and from which to test models, were not at his disposal ; he had to originate and construct, almost single-handed, every piece of apparatus used in his investigations. By the gleam of the lantern lit by his work it became first possible to trace a pathway in the darkness, whereon subsequent investigators, equipped with the more powerful searchlights of modern science, were able to open up an unexplored domain.

We are justified in calling Otto Lilienthal the Father of Gliding Experiments. Though his work was not followed up in his own country, Germany, yet it bore ample fruit in other countries, as witness the work of Chanute, Pilcher, Wright Brothers, Ferber and others. Indeed, the modern aeroplane, with all its astounding records of altitude and distance, is the lineal descendant of that ill-fated motor-glider which caused the death of Lilienthal, and unfortunately the death-roll which he headed is stretching out and ever growing as the number of those who "ride the wind" on aeroplanes is increasing, and their feats becoming more important.

But this very inheritance of disaster gives food for reflection, and it is permissible to speculate whether the development of dynamical flight would not have proceeded on different lines had Lilienthal been spared some more years of useful life.

There can be no doubt in the mind of any reader of Lilienthal's work that he was aiming at "economy" in the work required for flight. He is constantly calculating and holding up to our admiration and emulation the wonderful economy of nature as applied to the flight of the larger birds, and it is safe to assume that his gliding experiments were but a means to an end, viz. to familiarize us with the wave motion and eddies of the air ocean around us : to develop or train a special sense for these constant changes in wind pressure and direction. That wonderful mechanical creation, the wing of a bird, with its supporting and propelling properties, was his constant, though apparently unattainable, ideal. With an engineering equivalent to it, with partly beating wing, did he expect to ultimately solve the problem of mechanical flight. His successors were content to perfect his gliders, they stopped short at the tangible success of supporting planes and relegated the propelling function to the aerial screw propeller, admittedly an inefficient mechanical device, which can only be retained so long as we are content to move with the speed of an express train and content to risk the consequences. The few isolated attempts to construct machines with flapping wings were too crude to prove—as is assumed—the hopelessness of this principle, and more and more public attention crystallizes on the sensational achievements of mono and biplanes—wonderful and gratifying no doubt, but woefully neglectful of the demands of efficiency or economy.

Motors of from 26 h.p. to 200 h.p. are requisitioned to enable one or two men to "fly."

Had it not been for the marvellous possibilities of the explosion motor, we should have been forced to be more economical with our available motive-power, and in all probability should, by now, have opened a new direction of investigation along the lines so frequently urged by Lilienthal, namely, "Bird Flight."

Nature, though prolific, is ever economical, and it behoves us to strive likewise after economy in the dynamics of flight, by trying to emulate the great model, so constantly exhibited to us by nature, viz. the bird.

It is in the hope of stimulating afresh some careful experimenters to a renewed attack upon the wing problem, with its wonderful detail of structure, that the translator has urged the publishers to place Lilienthal's work before the English-speaking world.

A. W. I.

CONTENTS

b

X

LIST OF PLATES.

The Evolution.

AN important work monopolizes a man and, besides many other sacrifices, claims the whole personality. It fires the imagination of the child, and softly approaches its elected disciple in an alluring, toying way, appropriate to the serenity of child life. But gradually it draws the soul more firmly into its golden nets.

It fascinates the youth, and never relaxes its hold on the adult.

The glory of a great discovery or an invention which is destined to benefit humanity, appears to him the more dazzling the closer he approaches it; he perceives not the thorns in that crown, he heeds not its weight, but his whole life is shaped to attain it.

My late brother Otto and I were amongst those upon whom enthusiasm seized at an early age. A story which was then much read powerfully stimulated our susceptible minds: "The travels of Count Zambeccay," an aeronaut, who finally lost his life on the occasion of one of his balloon journeys.

More particularly was our interest awakened by the detailed description and instruction which, in the language of an animal fable, the stork imparts to the willow wren.

The small willow wren happens to meet the stork, and complains of fatigue; the latter, in his generosity, offers him a seat on his back, and during the ensuing conversation the stork explains the method by which he sails without effort or wing-beats, and how he planes down in a straight line from a great altitude to a distant meadow.

This clear description of sailing flight impressed us with the possibility of attaining such by simplé means.

Anklam, our native town, with its surrounding meadows, gave us ample opportunities for observation, since numerous families of storks had taken up their abode on the roofs of the barns, and we often watched the flight of the big, handsome birds. Our interest in the animal world also attracted us towards butterflies, and to complete our collection of these, which was the pride of our mother and ourselves, we did not shirk the weary miles to the "Karlsburgerheide," nor did we heed the gruesome nights spent in cemeteries, since there we found our rarest specimens. Still, we devoted the greater part of our immature nature studies to watching our friend the stork on the peaceful meadows of the "Karlsburgerheide." Often we would stalk him to within a very short distance and that with the wind, as his powers of scenting are but small, but on suddenly perceiving us he rose, hopping in our direction until sufficiently lifted by the force of his wings.

Even at that time it became obvious to us that rising against the wind must be easier than with the wind, because without some compelling cause the shy bird would not advance towards us.

In 1861 our father died; he had just prepared to emigrate to America, his mechanical aptitude finding no satisfaction in his business as a cloth merchant.

Our mother fostered in every way our mechanical proclivities, and never refused us the means to purchase the requisite materials for our experiments, however hard it may have been for her at times.

Well do I remember submitting to her our plans for our first flying machine, to the construction of which she readily consented.

Less encouraging was an apprehensive uncle, who constantly prophesied disaster.

Our first wings measured 2 metres by 1 metre, and consisted of thin beach veneer with straps at the undersides, through which we pushed our arms. It was our intention to run down a hill and to rise against the wind like a stork. In order to escape the jibes of our schoolmates, we experimented at night time on the drill ground outside the town, but there being no wind on these clear star-lit summer nights, we met with no success.

We were then 13 and 14 years of age respectively, and our flying experiments rather interfered with the proper discharge of our school work. We were both not particularly strong on Latin, and our mother therefore placed me in the "Realschule," whilst Otto, my elder brother, was sent to the Provincial Technical School at Potsdam.

Here Otto was able to satisfy his thirst for technical knowledge, and after a lapse of two years he passed the final examination with the highest honours ever attained by any previous scholar.

We had no associate in our aviation experiments; we felt ourselves quite equal to the task. During the vacations we returned to our old hunting grounds; buzzards, hawks, rooks, and storks interested us most, and great was our delight when we saw a swarm of swans outlined against the sky on their migration to their northern breeding grounds.

My brother left Potsdam for Berlin, and for one year worked as mechanic at the machine works of Schwartzkopf. He soon proved his great skill in exact mechanical work of any kind with which he was entrusted. After that he was sent to the Technical Academy, but before the commencement of the first term, he paid us a month's visit at Anklam.

He brought with him a bundle of palisander sticks, which were intended for flying machine No. 2. I was at that time apprenticed to an architect, and took a holiday in order to assist my brother.

To work the hard palisander wood was no small matter; we pointed and rounded the sticks which served as quills for two wings, 3 metres long each. The feathers of these quills were represented by a series of large goose feathers which were sewn on tape.

For this purpose we had purchased all the feathers which were obtainable in our town, and this is no mean accomplishment in any Pomeranean town.

The sewing on of these quills was very troublesome and fatiguing for the fingers, and many a drop of blood upon the white feathers testified to the damage done to our finger tips.

The wings were fastened to two hoops, one of which was strapped round the chest, and the other round the hips, and by means of an angle lever and stirrup arrangement to the ropes we were enabled to beat the wings up and down by pushing out our legs. The single feathers were arranged to open and close on the up-and-down stroke, and the arrangement worked perfectly. We felt sure that this time failure was impossible. We believed that the lofty garret of our house in Anklam would be the most suitable experimenting room, a belief which was unfortunate, since we undertook to fly in a perfect calm, a method which presents difficulties even to the bird.

We did not heed the lesson taught by our storks, but suspended our apparatus from the beams of the roof and began to move the wings. The very first movement of our legs brought about a jumping at the suspension rope, and as our position was nearly horizontal we were most uncomfortable. When drawing up our legs, that is, when the wings moved upwards, the whole arrangement dropped down and hung on the taut rope. The lifting effect due to the beating down of the wings amounted to 20 cm. This was at least some success, but if our house had not possessed that high loft, we should have experimented in the open, and with a fresh wind would have recorded better results. But the holidays and leave were at an end, and flying machine No. 2 was relegated to the lumber room.

In October of 1867 my brother Otto entered the Technical Academy in order to study engineering. Unfortunately it was impossible for him to obtain a scholarship, not even our Family Scholarship, because, according to the idea then obtaining, the Technical Academy was not a high school, and it was therefore necessary to manage with very little.

In 1868 I joined my brother in Berlin, in order to devote myself to the building trade, and we attained a real proficiency in the "simple life." A pennyworth of cherries and about the same amount of bread was our favourite lunch, but when finally, through the recommendation of Director Reuleaux, my brother obtained a yearly scholarship of 300 Thalers, we were able to live like princes on this fabulous sum. The first thing which we afforded was a large bundle of willow canes with which to construct flying machine No. 3. We had abandoned the use of hard palisander wood, because experiments showed us that, weight for weight, the round willow canes possessed the greatest resistance against breakage so long as its surface was intact, and that even with the latter defective, it still held together.

The disagreeable descent while lifting the wings, we were going to eliminate by arranging two larger and four somewhat smaller wings, which alternately moved upwards and downwards, and instead of the expensive quills we employed a kind of valve between the separate canes made of shirting, sewn to the tips of willow canes. The whole apparatus had an area of 16 sq. m., and weighed only 15 kg.

FIG. 1.—Glide at Südende (Start).

When everything was prepared, since we could not mount the

FIG. 2.—Difficult landing.

apparatus in our lodgings, we took it, during the holidays, to

Demnitz, an estate near Anklam belonging to our uncle. The experiments which we made with this apparatus are described in § XVI. of the present volume.

The exigencies of our studies, for the time being, terminated our experiments. When the war of 1870 commenced, my brother Otto took the field; his comrades often spoke of their chum, who, even during the campaign never lost sight of the great object of his life, namely, the problem of flight. Full of plans he returned from the war, and I met him the day before the great entry of the troops in Berlin. His first words were, "Now we shall finish it,"

FIG. 3.—Glide at Südende.

but matters did not develop quite so quickly. After he had left the service, we worked together in Berlin. We had now come to the conclusion that flight would be impossible without forward motion, and all the experiments which we made on small models were based upon the principle of forward motion. We possessed an apparatus which was fitted with beating wings, moved by spiral springs and which was launched from an inclined plane out of the window of our lodging on the fourth floor, at 4 o'clock in the morning, so as to avoid being seen.

The centre of gravity of this apparatus was too low, and the resulting pendulum movements brought the wings almost into a vertical position and to rest; the apparatus swung back and in consequence of the oblique position of the feather-shaped valves

FIG. 4.—Gliding Flight at Südende.

it took a second and third start until the spring had run down.

FIG. 5.—Gliding Flight at Gr.-Lichterfelde.

This experiment for the first time taught us the importance of the proper position of the centre of gravity.

The best of our various models was fitted with two pigeon's wings; it was able to make 20 wing-beats when the spring was wound up, and when pushed off gently, flew across two rooms.

Otto Lilienthal now commenced his business career. His first situation was in the engineering works of Weber, then under the management of the present Geheimrat Rathenau. After some time he took a position as designer in the engineering works of C. Hoppe.

There was now a longer interval in our flying experiments. In his spare time Otto took up the calculation of hot air motors and

FIG. 6.—Glide at Südende (Dangerous Position).

actually commenced a model without, however, finishing it. At this time, I was travelling in Austria and England, whilst Otto lived with our grandmother and sister; we lost our mother in 1872. In 1874, when I returned from England to Berlin, we again resumed our work on flight. In our loft we installed a regular workshop and laid the keel of a wing flyer. The wings were an exact copy of a bird's wings: the pinions consisting of willow canes with narrow front and wide back feathers. The latter we made of corrugated paper steeped in a solution of gum arabic, and after drying, it was covered with collodion. The whole apparatus was the size of a stork, and the propelling force was to be a light motor which, however, had first to be designed. It was on this occasion that my brother Otto, who was experienced in the designing of steam-engines, invented a system of tubular boilers, then quite new. The engine was provided with a high and a low pressure cylinder, the former for the downstroke and the latter for the upstroke of the wings. I believe we should have succeeded in making the model fly, if the motor had not been too powerful, but at the very first trial both wings were broken, not being strong enough to withstand the increased air pressure due to the beating motion. Still we were not discouraged by this accident, which we considered as a success for the small motor. The latter with

FIG. 7.—Glide with Biplane from the Hill at Gr.-Lichterfelde.

some water and a supply of spirit weighed 0·75 kg. and had an output of $\frac{1}{4}$ h.p. We also built kites in the form of birds, in order to study the behaviour of the apparatus in the wind; the surfaces of the wings being curved, in order to imitate a bird. Such a kite, which we flew on the high plain between the Spandau Road and the railway to Hamburg, showed some peculiar properties. It was held by three persons, one of whom took hold of the two lines which were fastened to the front cane and to the tail, respectively, whilst the other two persons each held the line which was fastened to each wing. In this way it was possible to regulate the floating kite, as regards its two axes. Once, in the autumn of 1874, during a very strong wind, we were able to so direct the kite that it moved against the wind. As soon as its long axis was approxi-

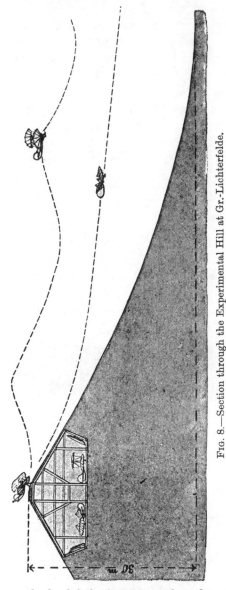

FIG. 8.—Section through the Experimental Hill at Gr.-Lichterfelde.

mately horizontal the kite did not come down but moved forward at the same level. I held the cords controlling the longitudinal axis, and my brother and my sister each one of the cords for the adjustment of the cross-axis. As the kite maintained its lateral equilibrium, they let go the cords; the kite then stood almost vertically above me and I also had to free it.

After another thirty steps forward my cords got entangled in some bushes, the kite lost its balance, and in coming down was destroyed. Yet, having gained another experience, we easily got over the loss of model No. 4. Our business duties as employees, with late office hours, prevented us from occupying ourselves with the subject more intensely. My brother Otto was then travelling frequently and for prolonged periods in order to introduce new machinery in mines. He had observed the slow method of bringing up coal and suggested to his chief an improvement which would facilitate the work of the miner. He constructed a special machine, and his firm, who could not take up this particular branch, gave him a prolonged leave to enable him to push the sale of this machine on his own account.

This brought him into the various mining centres of Saxony, Silesia, Tyrol, Hungary, and Galicia. He obtained some orders, especially from Austria, but as the coal trade was then bad, and whole mountains of coal were stored on the wharfs, there was little inducement to buy machines which were to expedite the work. His attempt to obtain an independent position was therefore a failure.

My brother made the acquaintance, during one of his journeys in Saxony, of his wife Agnes, née Fischer, the daughter of a mining official, and married her in 1878. Shortly before this, our grandmother was taken from us, and my sister had taken a position in England as a teacher. I lived for two years with the newly married couple, and during that time we invented the " Anchor " brick-boxes which became so well known in later years, and the joy of innumerable children, but which caused us much annoyance, worry, and still more monetary loss.

Disappointed by all this trouble, I collected my belongings and emigrated to Australia, whilst my brother Otto developed a system of tubular boilers for which he obtained a German patent. The invention was a timely one, for at that period only very inferior small motors were in existence. The freedom from danger of these tubular boilers was soon recognized by the authorities, and my brother was able to give up his position at Hoppe's and to start for himself.

We kept up a regular correspondence and frequently ventilated the problem of flight. The report of my journey dated from Cape Town contained the detailed description of the flight of the Albatross: " the Albatross is exactly the same shape as that of our kite, but its wings are still more narrow." During this time (1881–1886) we made no experiments. I had, as similarly related of the brothers Wright, endeavoured to construct on a larger scale the small flyers moved by a rubber spring, then much patronized and known as Japanese flies. But the result of our experiments was as negative as that of the Americans.

Soon after my return from Australia in 1886, Otto's business had yielded him sufficient to permit his building a home of his own

in Gross-Lichterfelde and we resumed our flight experiments,
which were facilitated by a nice laboratory and a large lawn. We
now commenced the fundamental experiments for the investigation
of air pressure given in the present volume, and we continued
them until the year 1893.

Whilst this book was still in the press, my brother Otto decided
to compare the actual lifting power of larger curved surfaces with
the values which we had determined by measurements. These
supporting surfaces are here illustrated, and are now generally

Fig. 9.—Albatross seen from below (one-thirtieth actual size).

termed "Gliders." We were able to slowly glide downward
against the wind from a height.

Our garden having many trees in it, was frequently without
wind, and we therefore transferred the field of our experiments to
the ground behind the Military Academy and later on to Gross-
Kreuz on the line of the Magdeburg railway. Here we found
that the wind was too changeable near the ground, so my brother
built a shed on the brink of a gravel pit in Südende, and there
was able to considerably extend his gliding flights.

In 1894, we had at considerable expense a special hill (15

metres high) constructed, at the Heinersdorfer Brick-works near Gross-Lichterfelde. The summit of this hill was formed by a shed in which our gliders were stored. Several of our illustrations show the glides from this hill. In the meantime we had discovered a very suitably situated ground near Rinow and Stöllen between Neustadt on Dosse and Rathenow. There, there are a number of bare sandhills which rise up to a height of 50 metres above the surrounding plain, and from this starting point my brother succeeded in making glides up to 350 metres in length.

The starting point was only at half the height of the hill because at the summit the wind was generally too strong. According to my observations the drop of this gliding flight amounted to eighteen metres. On the occasion of one such flight one of the supports for the arm broke, so that the apparatus lost its balance and fell from a height of 15 metres, but the special shock absorber which was fitted to the apparatus, prevented my brother from getting seriously hurt. In 1896 we had three years of such flights behind us, and in my opinion we could not expect any better results. We therefore intended to take up experiments with an apparatus fitted with beating wings, the latter being moved by means of a carbonic acid motor. We had already tested the apparatus as a mere glider without a motor, the latter requiring some improvements; my brother Otto was of the opinion that these gliding flights would develop into a sport. He was therefore indefatigable, and always anxious, to obtain greater security, and also hoped to derive some pecuniary benefit from these glides. Our experiments at Stöllen imposed upon us great expense, and altogether we had spent more money on these flight experiments than, from a mere business point of view, we could afford. We had agreed that on Sunday the 9th August we should for the last time travel to Stöllen in order to pack up the apparatus. I was prevented from this by an accident with my cycle. Our families whom we intended to take with us remained at home and my brother drove out accompanied by a servant. He intended to make some change on the rudder, but at the very first glide, the wind being uncertain, the apparatus when at a considerable height lost its balance.

Unfortunately my brother had not fitted the shock-absorber and the full shock of the fall took effect, so that the apprehension of our uncle was fulfilled. My brother fell, a victim to the great idea, which—although at that time was so little recognized—is now acknowledged in its full bearing by the whole civilized world. Our work has already produced good results and, combined with the development of light motors, the lifting power of curved surfaces has been fully confirmed.

Therefore, whenever the laurels of success are attained by an aviator of the present day, let him remember with grateful acknowledgment the work of Otto Lilienthal!

§ I.—Introduction.

WITH each advent of spring, when the air is alive with innumerable happy creatures; when the storks on their arrival at their old northern resorts fold up the imposing flying apparatus which has carried them thousands of miles, lay back their heads and announce their arrival by joyously rattling their beaks; when the swallows have made their entry and hurry through our streets and pass our windows in sailing flight; when the lark appears as a dot in the ether and manifests its joy of existence by its song; then a certain desire takes possession of man. He longs to soar upward and to glide, free as the bird, over smiling fields, leafy woods and mirror-like lakes, and so enjoy the varying landscape as fully as only a bird can do.

Who is there who, at such times at least, does not deplore the inability of man to indulge in voluntary flight and to unfold wings as effectively as birds do, in order to give the highest expression to his desire for migration?

Are we still to be debarred from calling this art our own, and are we only to look up longingly to inferior creatures who describe their beautiful paths in the blue of the sky?

Is this painful consideration to be still further intensified by the conviction that we shall never be able to discover the flying methods of the birds? Or will it be within the scope of the human mind to fathom those means which will be a substitute for what Nature has denied us?

Though neither the one nor the other of the above propositions has thus far been proved to be correct, we perceive with satisfaction that the number of those is increasing who have made it their task to shed more light on this dark pathway of knowledge.

The observation of nature constantly revives the conviction that flight cannot and will not be denied to man for ever.

No one who has had an opportunity of observing large birds,

B

which move through the air with slow wing-beats and often only with extended but motionless wings, especially the large birds on the high seas; of studying their flight at close quarters; of appreciating the beauty and perfection of their movements; of admiring the efficiency and safety of their flying apparatus; and who is able to deduce from the majesty of those movements the moderate efforts and, with the assistance of the wind, the small amount of energy required for such flight, can believe that the time is far distant when our knowledge and understanding of the method of flight will enable us to break the spell which has so far made it impossible to free our foot from mother earth even for one voluntary flight.

It must not remain our desire only to acquire the art of the bird, nay, it is our duty not to rest until we have attained to a perfect scientific conception of the problem of flight, even though as the result of such endeavours we arrive at the conclusion that we shall never be able to transfer our highway to the air. But it may also be that our investigations will teach us to artificially imitate what nature demonstrates to us daily in birdflight.

Therefore let us investigate in a truly scientific spirit, without preconceived notions as to the nature of birdflight, its mechanism, and the conclusions which may be derived from it.

§ II.—The Fundamental Principle of Free Flight.

The observation of flying creatures shows that it is possible by means of peculiarly shaped wings, which are moved through the air in a definite manner, to maintain heavy bodies floating in the air and to move them in any desired direction with great rapidity.

The bodies of flying creatures are not so materially lighter than those of other animals, as to justify us in considering this difference in weight an essential condition of flight.

It is often asserted that the hollow bones of birds facilitate their flight, especially since the hollows are filled with heated air, but it does not require much thought to come to the conclusion that this diminution of weight is barely worth mentioning. Also, we have not been able as yet to prove that the muscie and bone substance, as well as other parts of the bird's body, are specifically light.

Probably the feathery covering of the bird which gives it the appearance of greater bulk, especially if the feathers do not closely adhere to the body (as after death), is responsible for this assumed lightness.

After a bird is plucked, no one will assert that it is proportionally lighter than other animals, and our housewives are certainly not under the impression that a pound of bird's flesh, even with the hollow bone included, is more bulky than an equal weight of flesh from another animal. If, therefore, we add the weight of the feathers to that of the plucked bird, it does not make it lighter, but heavier, since feathers are heavier than air.

Hence, the feathery covering, whilst enabling the bird to spread its wings, and whilst rounding and smoothing off its body for the easier passage through the air, cannot be considered a special factor which would aid him in rising into the air.

We must assume that the free ascent from the ground, the hovering in the air, as well as the rapid movement through the air, of flying creatures, is the result of certain mechanical actions which may possibly be artificially imitated, and which by means of suitable mechanical arrangements, may be applied to creatures which are not intended by nature for flight.

The element of the flying creature is the air. The very small density of air does, however, not permit them to float and swim in this element as fishes do in water, but only a constantly maintained action between the air and the sustaining surfaces or wings of flying creatures, often accompanied by great muscular effort, prevents the falling down of the bird.

Yet, this small density of the air which makes a free ascent difficult, on the other hand is of great advantage to these creatures. For instance, the ease with which the air may be traversed on account of its small density, enables many birds to fly forward with extraordinary rapidity, and we have records of flight velocities, especially for some birds, which astonish us, exceeding by far as they do the velocity of the fastest express trains. Once artificial flight has enabled us to rise from the ground, it does not appear difficult to attain great speed in the air itself.

However, we should not consider rapidity of flight as the main thing to be aimed at, but rather the ability to prevent falling, since the former factor follows almost automatically as soon as the conditions for the latter are attained.

Flying creatures, and especially birds, demonstrate that transit through the air is far more perfect than all other modes of locomotion to be found in the animal kingdom as well as any method of artificial locomotion devised by man.

True, there are animals on land and water which have been endowed by nature with considerable speed, partly to enable them to pursue their prey, and partly to escape from their pursuers; speeds which often compel our admiration; but what are these accomplishments compared to those of the birds?

It is comparatively nothing for the stormy petrel to describe circles measuring miles around the ocean greyhound, and to come up with the ship within a few moments after having fallen back for miles.

Brehm, our prominent observer of bird life, grows enthusiastic in describing the endurance of the large sea birds. He considers it proven that such a bird follows for hundreds of miles in the wake of the steamer during day and night, only resting a short time on the water and never resting on the ship itself.

These birds appear to find their support in the air itself, since they are not only flying during the daytime but even at night. And they seem to utilize the sustaining powers of the wind in so perfect a manner that their own efforts are barely required. Yet they are always where they desire to be as though their volition was the only motive for their flight.

To make this most perfect of all modes of locomotion his own has been the aim of man from the beginning of history. In thousands of ways man has tried to equal the performance of birds. Wings without number have been made, tested, and rejected by mankind, but everything has been in vain and we have not attained this much desired aim. Actual voluntary flight is even to-day as much of a problem for humanity as it was thousands of years ago.

The first voluntary rise of man into the air was effected by means of balloons. The balloon is lighter than the air it displaces and is therefore able to lift other objects which are heavier than air. But the balloon presents under all circumstances, even in its elongated, pointed form, such a large area in the direction of motion and meets with such great resistance in its passage through the air, that it is not possible to propel it through the air, especially against the wind, with such velocity that it equals the voluntary rapid locomotion observed in flying creatures.

It is, therefore, evident that in order to approach the splendid attainments of flying creatures, we must forego entirely the assisting effect of the buoyancy of gases lighter than air, that is to say, give up the balloon and employ a principle of flight in which only very thin surfaces come into consideration, which offer very little resistance to the air in passing through it in a horizontal direction.

Flying creatures are able, by applying this principle, to lift themselves into the air and to progress rapidly through it, and if we desire to utilize the efficiency of this principle, we must necessarily discover the correct explanation of such effects.

The investigation of these causes must include the mechanical problems which govern flight, and thus dynamics, i.e. the knowledge of the action of forces upon matter, will be the means of explaining these phenomena.

The necessary reasoning is of a comparatively elementary nature, and it is of advantage to consider for a moment the relation between flight and dynamics.

§ III.—The Art of Flight and Dynamics.

The dynamics of birdflight have to take into account chiefly those forces which affect the flying bird. Flying is nothing more than a constant opposition to that force with which the earth attracts all bodies, including living creatures.

The flying bird, by means of its flight, overcomes this attraction and does not fall to earth, although he is as much subject to the effect of gravitation as any other creature.

Terrestrial attraction or gravity is part of a natural law which applies to the whole universe and in virtue of which all bodies attract each other. This attraction increases with the mass of the bodies and decreases with the square of their distance apart, such distance to be measured between their respective centres of gravity.

Though a bird may rise higher and higher into the air, we cannot consider that the force of gravity acting upon him is thereby diminished, because the distance by which he rises is negligible in comparison with the initial distance of the bird from the centre of gravity or the centre of the earth.

Since our proximity to earth is so very great, relative to our proximity to other heavenly bodies, we can only trace the force of gravity which attracts us to earth.

The weight of the body is the force with which the earth attracts this body, and as the unit of force the weight of 1 kg. has been accepted, and all other forces are measured in terms of this.

In dynamics we figuratively represent a force by a straight line in the direction of the force, and give this line a certain length, corresponding to the magnitude of the force.

Gravity is represented by a vertical line directed towards the centre of the earth, and like all other forces, can only be recognized by its visible effect, which is the production of movement.

When a force acts uniformly on a free body which is at rest, it begins to move in the direction of this force and to increase steadily in speed. The velocity at each instance is measured by the distance traversed during one second. If the movement during this second is uniform, we call this distance the velocity of the body.

The attraction of the earth or gravity would impart to a bird in the air which is suddenly deprived of its ability to fly a movement directed vertically downward, the velocity of which would uniformly increase, and the bird would fall until he is in contact with the earth. But such a fall in air does not give an exact idea of the magnitude of gravity, since the resistance of air modifies the velocity as well as the direction of the fall.

The true effect of gravity can only be demonstrated in a vacuum, because then every object, irrespective of its properties, falls with the same uniformly increasing velocity ; at the end of the first second it has attained a velocity of 9·81 metres, a velocity which uniformly increases by 9·81 metres during every additional second.

This increase of velocity per second is called the acceleration, so that gravity has an acceleration of 9·81 metres.

This acceleration becomes apparent during the normal flight of the bird. When raising his wings for a new beat, gravity immediately becomes effective, and the bird falls by a short distance until the new wing-beat lifts the bird by a distance equal to the previous drop, and so counterbalances the effect of gravity.

Gravity is, however, not the only force which acts upon the bird, and he really owes his ability to fly to the existence of various other forces by which he counteracts the effects of gravity.

In dynamics we distinguish propelling forces and restraining forces or resistances.

Propelling forces include, besides gravity, the muscular power of all living creatures, the expansion of water vapour under pressure, and the expansion of elastic springs.

Every propelling force may, however, appear as a restraining force when it acts on a body in a sense contrary to the direction of the movement of this body, and in this way diminishes the movement, as, for instance, in the case of the effect of gravity on an object which has been thrown into the air.

One of the latter forces is that which nature utilizes so perfectly in the process of birdflight, and which we shall study more particularly in the present volume: the so-called "resistance of the medium" which affects every body which is moved in the medium, for instance, in air.

Such a resistance can never act as a propelling force, because it is only created by the motion itself, and always endeavours to diminish this motion until it ceases to be.

The resistance of a medium, for instance, that of the water or that of the air, can only indirectly become a propelling force, namely, when the medium itself is in motion; examples of this are seen in water-wheels, wind-mills, and, as we shall see later on, sailing birds.

Further examples of restraining forces are friction and the cohesion of solid bodies. These likewise cannot directly act as propellants, but only as resistances which have to be overcome; for instance, friction when moving weights, and cohesion when working wood, metals, or other solid bodies, in which case the cutting tool has to overcome the cohesion.

Force is always to be considered as the cause of a motion, but if a body is at rest we must not conclude that it is not under the influence of forces; for instance, if a body rests on a support, gravity still acts upon it, but its effect is nullified because it is opposed by several forces of equal magnitude acting in the opposite direction, namely, the reactive pressure of the support which acts just as strongly upon the body from below as the body presses upon the support by virtue of its weight. If both acting forces balance each other, the body is said to be in static equilibrium. A similar supporting force must act upon the bird floating above, a force which the bird must have created in some manner and which balances its weight.

The effective forces combine on a flying bird according to the principles of dynamics, so that when they act in the same direction their effect is added together, and when they act in opposite directions they will either wholly or partly compensate each other according to their respective magnitudes. Forces which do not act in the same direction on the bird's body can be combined according to the rules of the parallelogram of forces, just as we are able to resolve one force into two or several forces which have the same collective effect as the original force. The movements produced by the forces do not differ in any way when applied to birdflight.

When a force has imparted motion to a body and then ceases to act, or if another force begins to act which balances the first force, the body will continue in motion with the same velocity and in the same direction which it had when the last single force acted upon it. It is then said to be in dynamic equilibrium, and although there is motion, no further force acts upon it.

A bird, when flying with uniform velocity, is in such an equilibrium. There is a perfect balance between the forces because the bird not only produces by its wing-beats a force which equalizes that of gravity, but it also overcomes continuously that resistance which the air opposes to the passage of the body through it. The moving of a lathe or a grinding-stone by means of a treadle in order to work metals, and the use of the muscular power of our legs to overcome cohesion and friction, appears a simple process; no less simple, when properly analysed, is the reasoning which has enabled us to convert the potential energy stored in fuel into steam-power in order to overcome resistances which are beyond our muscular powers.

The time may come when the technique of aviation will represent an important branch of industrial work; when the gulf between mere theory and actuality has been bridged; when the first man has clearly recognized those means which will make the employment of powerful motors superfluous, and will undertake his first voluntary flight through the air.

Whether that man then understands how to utilize to the fullest his flying apparatus so that his muscular power suffices for the necessary movement, or whether he has resource to engine-power in order to push his wings with the necessary force through the air; in either case his will be the merit of being the first fighter in that struggle for the realization of the power requisite for flight.

It is absolutely necessary that we should obtain some idea of the magnitude of this effort; only when we have become fully acquainted with this can we seek for means of solving that great problem.

What is "effort"? What do we understand by "work done during flight"? These definitions must have the same meaning for flight as for other problems of mechanics.

Every force which produces a visible effect does "work;" overcoming any resistance requires "work."

"Work" is necessary in order to lift a number of bricks on to the scaffolding; it is "work" which is necessary to pump water from the ground; "work" is required to mix the mortar with the water; and finally "work" must be done in order to beat a wing through the air.

The magnitude of this work depends upon the magnitude of the force expended, or upon the amount of resistance to be overcome.

It also depends upon the distance through which this force has to act or through which resistance is encountered.

"Force" and "distance" are therefore the factors which constitute "work," and the product of these two factors gives us a measurement of the work done.

We call this product of force and distance "*mechanical work*," and as a rule we express the force in kilograms, and the distance in metres, and their product in kilogrammetres (kgm.).

The rate at which such mechanical work is done depends upon the magnitude of the forces in operation, and the time requisite for a certain work is a measure of the energy doing the work.

As a unit of this energy we take the work done during one second, and we compare it with the average energy which a horse is capable of exerting in a second.

A horse can exert in one second a force of 75 kg. over a distance of one metre, and its energy is 75 kgm., and so long as their product is 75 kgm., the magnitude of force and velocity per second is unimportant.

This energy we call a " horse power," and denote it by "h.p." The energy which man is capable of rendering for prolonged periods is about ¼ h.p. For short periods man can do considerably more work, especially when able to make use of the strong muscles of the leg, as for instance when mounting staircases.

On easy staircases it is possible to lift one's weight per second a distance of one metre. A man weighing 75 kg. therefore renders an energy of 1 h.p. When considering the magnitude of any mechanical work, only the magnitude of the forces to be overcome and the distance traversed per second in the direction of the force (or the velocity) is of importance; the direction of the force is not important because it is easy, by simple mechanical means, to modify it at will.

It only requires a reference to the lever action of the wings and to the laws governing the moment of forces, as to which the air pressure on the wings comes to an expression, to show that the art of flight may be considered a purely mechanical problem, the analysis of which will be the subject of the following sections.

§ IV.—The Force which lifts the Bird in Flight.

The problems why a flying bird does not drop to the ground, how it is sustained in air by an invisible force, may be considered fully solved so far as the nature of this supporting force is concerned.

We know that this can only consist of the air resistance produced through the movement of the bird's wings.

We also know that the magnitude of this force must at least equal the weight of the bird, whilst in direction it must oppose gravity, *i.e.* it must act from below upwards.

Since the bird, whilst in flight, is not in contact with any other body than the surrounding air, the lifting force must have its origin in the air, the properties of which must be responsible for the support of the flying bird.

This sustaining force, which is produced by wing movements and muscular effort, can therefore be nothing other than the resistance of the air, *i.e.* the force which every body must overcome when moving through the air, or the resistance which opposes such movement. It is likewise the force with which air in motion or wind acts upon bodies in its path.

We know that this force increases with the sectional area of the moving or resisting body, and still more with the velocity of motion of such body or the wind.

Such air resistance will also be encountered by the bird's wing when beating downwards, and will act from below upwards, but only when the velocity of the wing has attained a sufficient magnitude will this resistance be sufficiently large to prevent the fall of the bird.

The lifting of the wings must take place under such conditions that the resulting air-resistance is incapable of pressing the bird as far down as the downward beat lifted it.

For the time being we may assume that before the upward stroke the wings execute such rotation as will offer the minimum of resistance to the air, or that the feathers in their altered position will permit the air to partially escape through them, and thus reduce the resistance to the air.

Whatever depressing effect the lifting of the wings may produce must be compensated for by a surplus of lifting effect due to the down stroke.

All this proves that, as above stated, the resultant force from the wing-beats of a bird in flight, must be an air resistance of a magnitude at least equalling the weight of the bird, and directed upwards.

§ V.—General Remarks on Air Resistance.

In moving a body through air, the particles of air in front of the body are pushed aside and forced to follow certain paths; the air behind the body being also set in motion.

If the body possesses a uniform velocity with regard to the air at rest, the motion of the air caused by the passage of the body through it will be uniform likewise and be mainly confined to opening out in front of the advancing body and joining up again in its rear. The air behind will partly share in the movement of the body, but besides certain regular eddying movements will be produced in it which persist for some time in the path described until by mutual friction they gradually subside.

These various movements must be imparted to the air which was initially at rest, and this accounts for the resistance opposed by the air to the movement of any object through it, a resistance which necessitates the expenditure of an equal force.

Our exact knowledge of this air resistance is unfortunately confined to only a few very simple practical cases, indeed we may say that only that air resistance is generally known which is produced when we move a thin, plane surface in a direction at right angles to its plane. But if the angle between direction of movement and plane differs from 90°, we find such a divergence between the formulæ given in various technical handbooks as to shake our confidence in their value.

Still less familiar are we with the air resistance of curved surfaces.

The only sufficiently proved and often demonstrated law shows that the air resistance is proportional to the area and to the square of the velocity.

A plane surface of 1 sq. m. which has a uniform velocity of 1 m. perpendicular to its plane is subject to a resistance of practically 0·13 kg.

Therefore the air resistance L in kg. of a surface of F sq. m., when moved with a velocity of v m., equals—

$$L = 0{\cdot}13\ Fv^2$$

It is obvious that the direction of this resistance is perpendicular to the plane; the point at which it may be considered to act on the plane is the centre of gravity of the latter.

It must be borne in mind that this formula is only correct when the velocity is uniform, *i.e.* when the phenomena in the surrounding air have become stable, a condition which is not applicable to wing motions, as we shall see later on.

The scarcity of data in technical works regarding air resistance may be due to the former absence of necessity for their exact knowledge, and only the advent of researches on flight shows up this gap.

§ VI.—The Wings considered as Levers.

The wing of a bird, moving up and down, possesses different velocities at every point; near the body its velocity is nearly zero, and it increases towards the tips of the wings.

It follows therefore that the air resistance produced on different portions of the wings will vary.

Whilst aware of the fact that the total air resistance below the wings must at least equal the weight of the bird, we cannot say how this resistance is distributed over the various portions of the wing, since such distribution may be influenced by a variety of circumstances.

As the centre of the total air pressure acting upon a wing, we must choose that point which would produce with the resultant

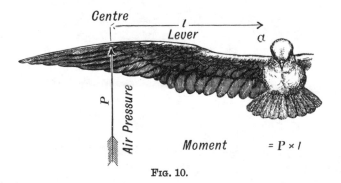

FIG. 10.

force of the air pressure and the lever l (distance from fulcrum a), Fig. 10, the same moment as the irregularly distributed lifting air resistance. At this point the air resistance would be concentrated if the wing were a perfectly stiff member, a fixed lever, which, however, in reality it is not. The bird would feel its support acting upon this point, but although not strictly true, yet the down-beat of the wings represents the same effort for the bird as though it had to overcome this air resistance acting at the end of that theoretical lever.

We must consider then that the real wing velocity which has to be produced by the muscular effort of the bird is the velocity of that point on which the centre of the air pressure acts.

For the calculation of the maximum stress (point a) the moment would be $P \times l$.

§ VII.—The Energy required for Wing Motion.

The bird feels the resistance opposed by the air to its wings, and the act of overcoming this resistance is the essence of the muscular energy expended by the bird in flight, especially when beating its wings downward.

The work done per second (energy) is the product of the force and the distance per second over which it is expended, *i.e.* the product of the air resistance produced by the wings into the velocity of the pressure centre.

The former being expressed in kilograms, and the velocity in metres, we obtain the result in kilogrammetres, 75 of which equal 1 h.p. Thus if we know the air resistance L (Fig. 11) produced by both wings, and the velocity of the points c, the muscular effort of the bird for flight may be accurately determined.

Supporting
Air Resistance

Fig. 11.

Let L average 3 kg., and assume that the velocity of the wing at the centre of pressure be 1 m., then the energy equals $3 \times 1 = 3$ kgm., or $\frac{1}{25}$ h.p.

This example is only intended to illustrate the connection between the energy required and the actual results achieved.

§ VIII.—The Actual Path of the Wings and the Sensible Wing Velocity.

Forward movement is the true aim and purpose of all flight, and it is therefore to be expected that the movement of a bird's wing not only consists of up and down strokes, but also simultaneously of forward strokes. This produces an absolute path and an absolute velocity for every part of the wing according to its inclination.

This absolute velocity does not, however, enter into the calculation of the energy required for wing motion, but only that component relative to the forward moving body, because the bird overcomes the tangible resistance to its wings only with that velocity with which it moves its wings relatively to its body. This movement only means exertion in so far as the wing muscles are contracted for this purpose only.

This relative velocity of the wings we may term the sensible velocity, and it alone enters into any calculation of the muscular energy required, however fast the bird may travel forward.

This velocity must not be directed vertically upward, and the lifting of the wings also, though to a lesser degree, will require effort; we must, however, exclude any component of wing velocity which does not enter into the calculation of the actual flight energy.

§ IX.—Apparent Effort of Birds.

An observation of birds in flight gives us a relative estimate of the effort required at any instant. The slower the wing motion and the less their amplitude the smaller evidently is the work expended. A bird circling or sailing with motionless wings obviously expends but very little muscular energy.

It is a comparatively easy matter to arrive at the numerical value of this energy; we can count the number of wing-beats per second, we may ascertain the weight of the bird and the shape of its extended wings; from the latter we are able to deduce the position of the centre of air pressure, and after observing the amplitude of the stroke we know the approximate lift of the pressure centre. These observations enable us to ascertain the "apparent flight effort of birds" with a fair amount of accuracy.

Let us assume that a bird moves its wings up and down with equal velocity, that the upstroke has a negligible effect upon the ascent and fall of the bird, and requires a negligible amount of work; the work necessary for flight consists then only in the downward beat of the wings, and only the distance through which the centre of air pressure travels per second relative to the bird itself must be taken into calculation.

A bird weighing G kg. will be pressed down by a force G during the upstroke of the wings, since gravity only acts upon it during that period.

In order to lift the bird again during the downward stroke of the wing as much as it dropped before, a lifting force of G kg. must be produced, and in order to produce this lift G, after deduction of the weight G, the down-beat of the wings must produce an air pressure of 2G. Only then can we imagine the flying bird to be in equilibrium, *i.e.* flying in a horizontal plane.

In reality the upstroke of the wings requires somewhat less time than the downstroke, so that the resultant air pressure need be somewhat less than 2G.

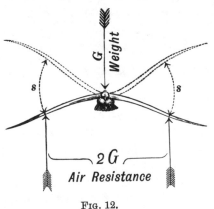

FIG. 12.

But for our approximate calculation we adhere to 2G, because we are then certain of having allowed for the small but nevertheless positive work required for the upstroke.

Fig. 12 represents the forces acting upon the bird during the downstroke of the wings.

This resistance must be overcome for the amplitude of the pressure centre (*s*) as many times as we count wing-beats per second (*n*).

The energy expended thus equals—

$$A = 2\ Gns.$$

Example.—A stork weighing 4 kg. is observed to execute two wing-beats per second, the amplitude of the pressure centre being about 0·4 m.

We have $G = 4$; $n = 2$; $s = 0·4$, and
$$A = 2 \times 4 \times 2 \times 0·4 = 6·4 \text{ kgm.}$$

or less than $\frac{1}{10}$ h.p.

Such an approximate calculation of the energy expended by various birds is most instructive, because it demonstrates the fact that it is much less than generally assumed.

The above calculation, though only an approximation, yields values which cannot differ very materially from the actual energy expended by birds.

§ X.—The Over-estimation of the Energy requisite for Flight.

The insufficient knowledge of the laws concerning air resistance gave rise to conceptions regarding the work done by birds in flight, according to which birds would be veritable monsters of muscular energy. It was not the velocity with which birds move their wings, but the area of the wings which was determined, and it was then calculated how fast they would have to move them in order to produce a sufficiently large air pressure.

For this purpose the usual formulæ to be found in technical handbooks were applied, and the resulting figures destroyed all hopes of ever imitating birdflight by mechanical means. An example will suffice.

Taking again the above-mentioned stork of 4 kg. weight as the subject of our calculation, and assuming it to have a wing area of about 0·5 sq. m., we should have to determine the wing velocity requisite to produce on its downstroke an air pressure of $2 \times 4 = 8$ kg.

Applying the general formula $L = 0\cdot13\ Fv^2$, we obtain—

$$8 = 0\cdot13 \times 0\cdot5 \times v^2$$

thus

$$v = \sqrt{\frac{8}{0\cdot13 \times 0\cdot5}} = 11 \text{ m. approx.}$$

since this velocity only acts during half of the flight time, we obtain as the *Energy*—

$$8 \times 5\cdot5 = 44 \text{ kgm., or more than } \tfrac{1}{2} \text{ h.p.}$$

Let us furthermore consider that in the above calculation we have assumed that every part of the wing is fully utilized and has a velocity of 11 m. If we were to introduce the actual wing movement the results would be still more startling, totalling more than 1 h.p., whilst in reality, as we have seen, and under the most unfavourable conditions of flight, only about $\frac{1}{10}$ h.p. is required.

This example will go far towards explaining the prevalent idea that the solution of the whole problem of flight would lie in the evolution of extremely powerful and light motors. An observation of nature, however, demonstrates that the expenditure of such enormous energies on the part of flying creatures must be relegated to fable, and impresses us with the conviction that there must be somewhere a Key to solve the problem.

§ XI.—The Work required for Various Kinds of Flight.

It must be conceded that birds are strong creatures, and that their organs of flight are endowed with muscles to a degree which is not often equalled by the organs of locomotion to be met with in other members of the animal kingdom; yet it seems improbable that birds are able to expend such energies as above calculated (a stork more than 1 h.p.), and according to our knowledge of the muscle substance it seems also impossible. The calculation, however, of the apparent energy required, which probably conforms much more closely to reality, presupposes for the muscular efforts of birds the possession of strongly developed muscles, but nothing unnatural.

Every careful observer of birds is aware that many birds are able to maintain themselves in the air, apparently sailing or floating without visible wing movements, and therefore without appreciable muscular effort; the majority of the birds of prey, swamp birds, and almost all the sea birds belong to this category. They make use of sailing flight, if not exclusively at least so frequently that we may draw our conclusions regarding the special suitability of sailing flight for certain methods of locomotion, or for certain conditions of the atmosphere.

At any rate it is a fact that, under certain circumstances, long-continued flight without appreciable wing motion is possible, and in many cases flight must be possible by means of suitable wings and with the expenditure of moderate mechanical effort, apparently less than that required for walking on the ground.

Only on this supposition can the endurance shown by some birds be explained. Many are actually on the wing during the whole day, from sunrise to sunset, and show no fatigue; our various species of swallows, who literally live in the air, are good examples. They seem only to alight when collecting material for building their nests. The tower swallow cannot even rise from the level ground, and only uses its rudimentary feet to scramble into its nest. How else could we imagine such a life in the air without assuming the work required for flight to be at least moderate? What would have to be the rate at which alimentary and respiratory functions make up for the motive energy required for such continuous flight according to the well-known equation for air pressure? We are here confronted by a problem, the elucidation of which will occupy us in the following sections.

The expenditure of such small energy is, however, not always possible in flight—for example, not in the case of rising from earth or water in a dead calm, or when hovering in still air. In these cases we notice that birds beat their wings much more energetically than usual, and we observe distinctly that such flight produces fatigue within a short time. But even this effort does not approach in magnitude those figures calculated in the preceding section, though furnishing an explanation for the presence of the powerful pectoral muscles.

According to the various kinds of flight we have to differentiate between the various requisite amounts of energy.

We have observed that rising in still air appears to necessitate a special effort on the part of the bird; there are many species of birds who are not able at all to rise from the level ground, and yet must be included amongst the most skilled and enduring of flyers.

Most of the smaller birds are able without moving forward to maintain themselves for a while stationary or even somewhat ascending in still air. This we may observe in sparrows who look for insects below the eaves.

But the possibilities of such flight are strictly limited.

It is known that a sparrow who has dropped into a chimney or shaft cannot leave it by vertical flight though the shaft be wide. Even when the side of such a square shaft is 2 m. long, sparrows are only able to fly up a few metres, and generally drop down again utterly fatigued. It is evident that in these cases they fail to attain the forward speed required for flight. From this and many other examples, stationary flight appears to call for the greatest exertion.

A comparison of the number of wing-beats tends to prove that a bird who is in rapid forward flight does less work than when commencing his flight, and simultaneously the amplitude of the wing movement decreases.

It is obvious that during forward flight certain forces must come into action which have their origin in the laws of air pressure, and explain that actual reduction in the energy required, which therefore are also the cause that even for slower and less pronounced wing-beats (requiring less work), that air pressure is produced which equals or surpasses the weight of the bird and produces a sufficient lift.

The advantage which forward flight offers to the bird is also given to him by a head wind. All birds therefore facilitate their rise by running against the wind even at the risk of having to pass the gun or jaws of their enemies; this is an important factor of which both man and bird are fully aware.

Many of the larger birds endeavour to attain the forward velocity requisite for rising by hopping in great jumps. Whoever has observed the efforts of cranes, etc., to rise in a calm will always remember these characteristic jumps accompanied by wing-beats.

Finally, there is a third kind of flight which we observe in birds, and for which there must be still less effort required, since the wings do not beat up and down at all, but are only slightly turned and tilted.

The bird appears to rest with his wings on the air, and only to improve his wing positions from time to time in order to accommodate himself to the air and the flight direction.

So far as we know a certain strength of wind is indispensable for such horizontal floating or spiral rising, because all birds when executing such manœuvres seek the higher strata in which the wind blows stronger and with less hindrance.

This is clearly demonstrated by certain birds of prey ascending in the clearing of a forest. They can only rise by means of laboured wing-beats, since in such a clearing a calm is usual, but as soon as they are on a level with the tree tops over which the wind can blow, they commence to describe their graceful curves. Their wings are at rest, and so far from falling, they raise themselves up higher and higher until lost to sight.

Such floating flight must not be confounded with the drifting on still wings which all birds indulge in by utilizing the momentum they have acquired, and rushing forward but gradually sinking and losing speed until settling on a support. The last stretch of such a path and the last remainder of momentum is often the means of producing a slight elevation when they choose for their support an object at a higher level than the ground.

We may now divide the movements of flight with regard to the necessary energy into three groups.

The first consists in flight without forward movement and without wind action, i.e. a condition in which the bird is relatively stationary with regard to the surrounding air. This would also apply when a bird flies with the wind, having the same velocity as the latter. In these cases the maximum flight work is required also when the bird desires to rise quickly and vertically.

To furnish this work the powerful muscles of the bird are utilized ; every bird has occasion, when rising and when hunting for food, to make use of these pectoral muscles ; he requires them in order to enter his element, the air, and to obtain food.

The second category is the one generally employed by birds

for their ordinary locomotion. It consists of the usual flight with moderately rapid wing-beats; all flying birds are capable of it, and, with the exception when flying against a strong head wind, it always signifies a rapid change of locality. Such flight requires moderate efforts on the part of the bird, and many species develop considerable endurance, from which we conclude that the muscles which come into play are not taxed to their utmost capacity.

The third class of flight must be called floating flight, and resembles a passive floating on air, active wing movements being absent.

Such flight seems to presuppose a certain favourable construction of the flying members, since only certain and generally larger birds are able to practise it.

This class commands our greatest interest because it proves that the solution of the problem of flight by man does not depend upon the provision of energy only; there is a method of flight requiring almost no effort, and being found more frequently among the larger birds.

To elucidate the principle of this kind of flight should be considered the supreme aim of the science of aviation, although it must also include the elucidation of the conditions of the other types of flight and their actual requirements of energy.

§ XII.—The Foundations of Flight Technique.

It is only by going back to fundamental researches that we may hope to promote the real knowledge of birdflight, and it is also necessary to start from the foundations of the technique of flight in order to study the perfect movements demonstrated by birds, and to imitate them artificially.

What we thus find must be of an extremely important nature in order to explain away the great contradiction which a calculation of the requisite flight energy presents.

How are those wings to be constructed, and how are they to be moved when we wish to imitate that which nature shows us in so masterly a fashion, when we desire to effect that rapid, voluntary flight which requires so small an expenditure of energy?

All flight is based upon *producing* air pressure, all flight energy consists in *overcoming* air pressure.

Air pressure must always be produced in sufficient magnitude, but we must overcome it with a minimum of velocity, so as to minimise the requisite energy.

This forces upon us the conviction that our knowledge of the actual mechanical processes of birdflight can only be increased by a successful research into the laws of air resistance, and that such knowledge will finally yield us the means of technical success. Birdflight is a method of flight which requires comparatively little energy, and only when we have found a true explanation of that shall we find the means for an exploitation of its advantages.

Therefore the laws of air resistance form the foundation of the technique of flight.

But the question arises, how are we to proceed in order to investigate these laws, and those properties of our atmosphere which we may use for the support of a body in free flight? A simple theoretical reasoning can produce supposition but no facts.

A simple practical experiment may result in positive data, but which, for their amplification, will require careful theoretical consideration, and it is obvious that only by a suitable combination of theory and practice can we hope properly to elucidate this unexplored domain of investigation.

The following sections are devoted to a consideration of the few available data.

Although this will not give us an exhaustive explanation of the various phenomena of birdflight, yet we may see that *natural birdflight utilizes the properties of air in such perfect manner, and contains such valuable mechanical features, that any departure from these advantages is equivalent to giving up every practical method of flight.* This applies, of course, in the first instance to the energy required, and it will depend upon the way this problem is solved by flight engineers whether we shall some day be able to utilize a means of locomotion such as we witness daily in birds.

§ XIII.—The Air Pressure on a Plane Surface moved perpendicularly and uniformly.

When a thin plane surface is moved with uniform velocity in a direction vertical to its area, we are assuming the simplest case for which a purely theoretical consideration, together with the knowledge of the density of air, gives us a result: a result which is in accordance with the data furnished by practical experiment.

It has been found that the air pressure increases in direct proportion to the *area* and in proportion to the square of the *velocity*, and also contains a constant which depends upon the density of the air and the resulting inertia. For our present purpose we may neglect the variations in air density produced by temperature and moisture, and apply the approximate equation—

$$L = 0 \cdot 13 \, F v^2$$

The configuration of the plane and its surface condition, whether smooth or rough, have been shown by experiments to be of negligible influence on the air pressure. The phenomena applying to such a uniform moving surface [1] have already been discussed in § V.

§ XIV.—Air Pressure on a Plane Rotating Surface.

The movement of a bird's wing resembles somewhat the rotation of a surface round an axis. For every line of such a surface parallel to the axis of rotation AA, BB (Fig. 13) a special air pressure exists, owing to the different velocity with which such lines move.

When a wing of length AB = C rotates round axis AA, and supposing the width of the wing to be constant, the specific air

---

[1] The expression "surface" is used to denote a solid but very thin surface.

pressure increases with the square of the distance from A. Dividing the wing parallel to AA into many equal strips, and plotting the air pressure on these strips as ordinates, their ends will be situated on a parabola AD (Fig. 15). The line passing through the centre of gravity of the area of this parabola (ABD), determines in C the centre of air pressure; this point, C, is to be found at $\frac{3}{4}$ $\mathfrak{L}$ from A. Another method of looking at this matter is shown in Fig. 15. In the same proportion as the ordinates of the parabola, increase also the sections of a pyramid and the weights of little truncated pyramids when we assume the pyramid to be sawn up parallel to its base, BBBB, into many equally thick slices. The centre of gravity of these slices likewise is the centre of gravity of the whole pyramid at $\frac{3}{4}$ $\mathfrak{L}$ distance from point A.

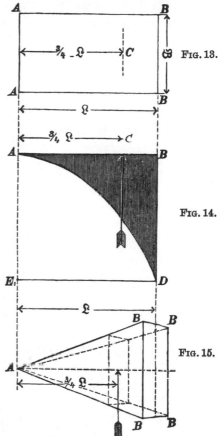

FIG. 13.

FIG. 14.

FIG. 15.

The total air pressure represented in Fig. 14 by area ABD, or in Fig. 15 by the pyramid, is $\frac{1}{3}$ of that pressure which would result from moving the whole area ABDE with the velocity of its edge B through the air.

If B stands for the width, $\mathfrak{L}$ for the length of the wing, and c for the velocity of BB, the air pressure will be—

$$W = \tfrac{1}{3} \times 0.13\ B\mathfrak{L}c^2.$$

Reduced to the angular velocity ω, and putting $(L^2\omega^2 = c^2)$, we have—

$$W = \tfrac{1}{3} \times 0.13\ B^2\mathfrak{L}^3\omega^2.$$

If, as in Fig. 16, a triangular wing ABD rotates round the base A, the air pressure is only $\frac{1}{4}$ of that which would result if the width $\mathfrak{B}$ were uniform over $\mathfrak{L}$, *i.e.* $\frac{1}{4}$ of the above pressure. Although the area of the triangle is $\frac{1}{2}$ of that of the above rectangle, the pressure drops to $\frac{1}{4}$, because the area is least where the movement is greatest (at the point).

Fig. 16.

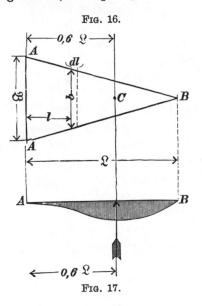

Fig. 17.

It is impossible to prove this equation by means of elementary analysis, and it has to be deduced as follows.

ω stands for the angular velocity; strip $b \cdot dl$ is subject to a pressure—

$$0\cdot13 \times b \cdot dl \omega^2 l^2.$$

Since $\qquad \mathfrak{B} = \dfrac{\mathfrak{L} - l}{b}$ or $b = \dfrac{\mathfrak{B}}{\mathfrak{L}}(\mathfrak{L} - l) = \mathfrak{B}\Big(1 - \dfrac{1}{\mathfrak{L}}\Big),$

the pressure is $\qquad 0\cdot13 \times \mathfrak{B}\omega^2\Big(l^2 \cdot dl - \dfrac{l^3}{\mathfrak{L}}dl\Big)$

Integrating for the whole area we obtain—

$$0\cdot13\mathfrak{B}\omega^2\int_0^{\mathfrak{L}}\Big(l^2 dl - \dfrac{l^3}{\mathfrak{L}}dl\Big) = 0\cdot13\ \mathfrak{B}\omega^2\Big(\dfrac{\mathfrak{L}^3}{3} - \dfrac{\mathfrak{L}^3}{4}\Big)$$

or the air pressure $W = \frac{1}{12} \times 0\cdot13 \times \mathfrak{B}\omega^2\mathfrak{L}^3$, *i.e.* $\frac{1}{4}$ of the pressure exerted upon a wing of uniform width $\mathfrak{B}$. The air pressure on strip $b \cdot dl$ has the moment $0\cdot13 b \cdot dl w^2 l^3$ with regard to the axis.

From this we obtain the total moment—

$$M = 0{\cdot}13\ \mathfrak{B}w^2\!\int_0^{\mathfrak{L}} \left(l^3dl - \frac{l^4}{\mathfrak{L}}dl\right) = \tfrac{1}{20} \times 0{\cdot}13\,.\,\mathfrak{B}w^2\mathfrak{L}^4$$

Dividing this equation by the force W, we find the lever $\dfrac{M}{W} = 0{\cdot}6\ \mathfrak{L}$.

The centre of pressure for triangular wings lies at a distance $0{\cdot}6\ \mathfrak{L}$ from the axis of rotation.

Fig. 17 represents the distribution of the air pressure over the whole wing area.

§ XV.—The Centre of Pressure on the Wing during the Downstroke.

The foregoing calculations give us the means of determining the centre of the pressure below the wing.

A bird's wing (Fig. 18), being more or less pointed in shape, may not be considered as a rectangle, yet it is not pointed enough to be taken as a triangle. For the rectangular wing of equal width and length $\mathfrak{L}$, the centre of pressure is situated at $0{\cdot}75\ \mathfrak{L}$, from the axis of rotation, and for the triangular wing this figure would be reduced to $0{\cdot}6\ \mathfrak{L}$. We shall, therefore, not commit any very great error in assuming for this actual wing in the case of a simple downward movement the value $0{\cdot}66\ \mathfrak{L}$, so that the distance of the centre of pressure from the shoulder joint is assumed to average $\frac{2}{3}$ of the length of the wing.

FIG. 18.

This presupposes that the rotatory movement of the wing in the shoulder joint is the only movement relative to the surrounding air. In the case of additional forward movement, the position of this pressure centre will be materially altered, as we shall see later on. The above value of $\frac{2}{3}\ \mathfrak{L}$ may, therefore, only be used for the calculation of the visible effort required to keep the bird floating in the surrounding air without locomotion.

It is necessary to point out that the centre of air pressure on wings in simple rotation *is not* that point, the velocity of which, when distributed over the whole area, produces an air resistance equivalent to the pressure generated by the rotation.

The knowledge of this pressure centre is only of value for the determination of the stress to which the wing is subjected, and for calculating the mechanical work done in moving the wing.

For the rectangular, rotating wing, Fig. 13, the equivalent wing, possessing in all points the velocity of C at right angles to its plane, would be $\frac{16}{27}$, and for the case shown in Fig. 16 the equivalent area would only be $\frac{100}{206}$ in order to attain the same air pressure.

For the wing of a bird which conforms to neither shape, the equivalent value would lie midway between the above figures, say at about $\frac{1}{2}$, *i.e.* half the wing area moved normally with the velocity of the pressure centre (at $\frac{2}{3}$ distance from the shoulder) would produce the same air resistance acting at the same lever as the simple rotating wing—always remembering the necessary absence of forward movement.

These cases are, however, of minor importance for determining the effort of flight, and we shall find that we have to devote our principal consideration to other and much more important features.

§ XVI.—Increasing the Air Resistance by Beating Movements.

We now have to investigate an important factor, the air pressure produced—as in the beating of wings—by imparting suddenly a considerable velocity to a surface previously at rest.

For such a type of movement the above investigations cannot hold good, since no time is available to allow the establishment of uniform stream lines and eddies. Also, air which wholly or partly follows the uniform motion of a surface will, thanks to its inertia, oppose the new motion.

This case may be considered as though the whole air in contact with the surface on both sides offers resistance by inertia and that on sudden motion it is compressed in front of and attenuated behind the surface, most intensely in close proximity to it and gradually arriving at the normal value; the ultimate pressure on the surface is the resultant of these two effects. Pure mathematics and dynamics would enable us to arrive at an approximate value even in this case, were it not for a new complication introduced by the fact that the velocity at each instant of such a suddenly moved surface varies and depends upon the mass inertia of the surface, and that the variations of the air resistance itself influence the change in speed, when the movement is due to a positive force.

Not less difficult will be the experimental determination of the instantaneous values of the air pressures for such beating movements, since it is a question of distances covered in a fraction of a second with irregular velocity.

One fact, however, experiment will establish. We may determine in certain cases the average air pressure resulting from a surface movement similar to the wing-beat of a bird; and although the instantaneous value of the air pressure for the various phases of the movement cannot be easily determined, we may at least establish the integral lifting effect.

In the years 1867 and 1868 the authors made such experiments, and their results have shown that beating movements *do* actually produce quite a different air pressure than the uniform motion of a surface.

Beating the air with a given surface, and with a mean velocity, we may register 9 and even 25 times the air pressure which would result from moving the same area uniformly with that velocity.

This shows that, in order to produce the same air pressure, the mean velocity of flapping or beating surfaces need only be $\frac{1}{3}$ to $\frac{1}{5}$ of that required for uniform motion.

If, therefore, we distribute a certain distance travelled by a uniformly moved surface over several wing-beats, we may take 3 or 5 times as long, and yet obtain the same air resistance, and move our surface 3 or 5 times slower than would have to be the case otherwise.

Therefore only $\frac{1}{3}$ or $\frac{1}{5}$ of the work per second is required to overcome the air resistance.

Such a movement is thus obviously a means of materially reducing the rate of work necessary to produce the lifting air pressure in flight. All birds who rise in still air from the ground, or who endeavour to maintain themselves stationary in it by powerful wing-beats, evidently profit by this fact.

Without this economizing property of wing-beats, many feats performed by birds could not be rationally explained.

This thorough utilization of the inertia of air by the beating movements of the wings is of the very greatest advantage to flying creatures.

It is an advantage inherent to the principle of birdflight,

Fig. 19.

which we lose as soon as we depart from this principle—as, *e.g.* by employing rotating propellers, which under all circumstances consume more energy than the beating bird's wing.

The following experiment will show that the principle is not a privilege of birds alone.

We constructed an arrangement (Fig. 19) consisting of a double system of wings; a pair of wide wings in the centre, and a narrower pair in front and behind, these mounted so as to revolve around a horizontal axis, and so connected that the wings on one side ascended when those on the other side descended, and *vice versâ*. Since the two narrow wings together equalled in area the broader middle wing, we obtained on each side the same lifting area. There was also a "feathering" action, which permitted the air to pass through the wings on their upstroke.

By alternately pushing down the feet, one half of the wing area descended, the other ascended against little resistance, as shown in the figure. The whole machine was suspended by means of a rope and pulleys from a beam, and was counterbalanced by a weight. If the counterweight was heavy enough we could lift ourselves by beating the wings.

This arrangement permitted us to determine the amount of "lift" produced with such an apparatus moved by man-power, and to ascertain the resulting air resistance.

After a little practice we were able to lift half our weight, so that a 40 kg. counterweight sufficed to just balance the machine and operator, weighing together 80 kg. The requisite effort, however, was so great that we could maintain ourselves at a certain level only for a few seconds. The area of each system (sustaining surface) was 8 sq. m.; we estimated the energy expended at 70–75 kgm., because a comparison of this energy with that necessary when quickly ascending some stairs produced the same fatigue.

We pressed down each foot with approximately 120 kg. a distance of 0·3 m. twice per second, so that the energy was $2 \times 0·3 \times 120 = 72$ kgm.

The travel of the centre of resistance was about 0·75 m., so that the foot pressure was reduced there to $\frac{0·3}{0·75} \times 120 = 48$ kg., of which, say, 4 kg. were absorbed in lifting the wings, leaving 44 kg. for the downstroke. The real lifting force was $44 - 4 = 40$ kg. as measured.

The mean velocity of the pressure centre was about 1·5 m., resulting, as above seen, in 40 kg. air resistance for the 8 sq. m. of surface.

Had we moved the same area with a uniform velocity of 1·5 m., the air resistance would have been $0·13 \times 8 \times 1·5^2 = 2·34$ kg., but since, owing to their hinged construction, the wings (which were broader at their tips) possessed different velocities in their several parts, the actual resulting resistance would have been 1·6 kg., which is $\frac{1}{25}$ part of the value we actually measured for the beating movement of the wings. To attain 40 kg. air pressure with uniformly rotating wings, the velocity of the pressure centre would have to be $5 \times 1·5 = 7·5$ m., and the requisite work likewise five times greater.

This example proves that the energy expended by birds who maintain themselves by flapping in a given position is very greatly overestimated, and is, indeed, only about $\frac{1}{5}$ of that calculated from the usual equation—

$$\mathfrak{C} = 0·13 \ Fv^2.$$

Regarding the design of the machine shown in Fig. 19, the ribs of the wings were made of willow canes, the other portions of the frame of poplar; the valves consisted of tulle, which was stiffened every 60 mm. by transverse ribs of thin willow cane (2–3 mm.). The whole flap was then painted with collodion.

Thus we obtained a very light, dense covering for the wings, which was very little sensitive against moisture. We would mention that previously we had constructed another apparatus for the same purpose, which, however, was only fitted with two wings, both being pushed down simultaneously by stretching both legs, and lifted by drawing up the feet and pulling with the arms. The efficiency of this early apparatus was essentially less than that of the machine shown in Fig. 19, because it seems against the natural tendency of man to utilize leg power by simultaneous movements of the legs in the same direction instead of pushing the legs alternatively.

In order to obtain a general equation for every case of wing-beat motion, we require a sufficiently large number of varying experiments; the number of beats, the amplitude of their movement, and the shape of the wings obviously influence the coefficient of such an equation, which probably increases more rapidly than in simple proportion with the area.

This supposition was forced upon us, when we observed that with smaller surfaces we could only obtain a nine-fold increase of the air resistance by " beating."

For these experiments we employed surfaces of about $\frac{1}{10}$ sq. m., and the arrangement shown in Fig. 20.

A weight, G, actuating a drum, R, with crank, K, imparted an oscillatory movement to the levers A and B, at their common end

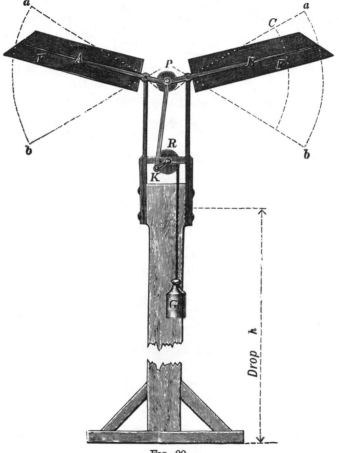

Fig. 20.

P, which, being a counterweight, balanced the weights of A, B, and the surfaces F, F.

During the descent of the weight G, the wings made a number of oscillations of amplitude, ab, for which they required a certain definite mechanical work, which in this case amounted to

$$G \times h \text{ kgm.}$$

D

This work was not only absorbed by the air resistance produced, but was partly utilized for setting the oscillatory masses in motion and overcoming the small friction.

This latter part may be separately ascertained by removing the wings, F, and replacing them by narrow battens of equal weight, fixed below A and B, having the same centres of gravity and the same moment of inertia with respect to the axis as the wings.

To obtain with this modified apparatus the same number of wing-beats per second, after thus eliminating the greatest part of the air resistance, a smaller weight, g, was sufficient.

By this we know that a weight equivalent to $G - g$ was used for the air resistance alone, the corresponding work being $(G - g)h$.

The air resistance itself is found by dividing this product by the amplitude of the excursion of the centre of pressure.

We have learned by previous experiments that this centre lies at a distance of $\frac{3}{4}$ wing-length from the axis, and that we only need to measure the excursion of the wings at this point, whilst the weight drops through a distance, h. Let this be w, then the mean air resistance equals—

$$\frac{(G - g)h}{w}$$

We have now to compare this with a case in which the wings travel distance w with uniform velocity for the same length of time by rotating in one direction. This resistance can easily be determined from the directions given in a previous section.

For instance, if the experimental surfaces were 20 cm. by 30 cm., $G = 2\cdot5$ kg., and $g = 0\cdot5$ kg., the drop $H = 1\cdot8$ m., and the time 6 seconds, the number of double oscillations 25, and the arc $ab = 32$ cm., then the centre, C, described an arc of $\frac{3}{4} \times 32 = 24$ cm., and in 6 seconds $2 \times 25 = 50$ times, thus a total distance of $50 \times 24 = 12$ m.

The work done was $(2\cdot5 - 0\cdot5) \times 1\cdot8 = 3\cdot6$ kgm., the air resistance thus—

$$\frac{3\cdot6}{12} = 0\cdot3 \text{ kg.}$$

On the other hand, by simply rotating the wings so that their centre likewise travels through 12 m. in 6 seconds, we obtain the corresponding resistance by remembering the $\frac{1}{3}$ rule.

The areas together are $2 \times 0.2 \times 0.3 = 0.12$ sq. m., or more accurately, after deducting the width of arms, A and B $- 0.11$ sq. m., the outer edges have a velocity of $\frac{4}{3} \times 2 = \frac{8}{3}$ m., and the air resistance is—

$$\frac{0.13 \times 0.11 \times (\frac{8}{3})^2}{3} = 0.033 \text{ kg.}$$

The proportion between the oscillatory and the uniform motion for the resulting resistance is—

$$\frac{0.3}{0.033} = 9.$$

For the last experiment we assumed a stiff surface, F, which gave the same resistance for up or down movement.

Substituting feathering surfaces, the upward resistance will be unequally disturbed for the up and down phase of the movements ; but the proportion between beating and uniform motion will be for small surfaces of $\frac{1}{10}$ sq. m., about 9 as before.

Although all this has proved the effect of beating motion upon the air resistance generally, we are not justified in concluding that the same proportion holds good for the actual wing-beats of a bird. We must not assume that the phases of movement produced by the muscular effort of the bird are identical with those produced in the above machines by gravity. But the advantage of this kind of wing movement and the consequent reduction of the energy required by the bird will be fairly obvious.

We may even calculate how much greater this advantage is in actual birds than in our experimental arrangements.

A pigeon weighing 0.35 kg. has a wing area of 0.06 sq.m., and beats its wings 6 times a second up and down; the amplitude of this movement measured at the centre of pressure being 25 cm. All this in calm air and without appreciable forward movement of the bird. Since the pigeon only takes about half the time for lifting its wing, the downstroke of the wings must produce a lift equal to the double weight $= 0.7$ kg.

The downstroke lasts $\frac{1}{12}$ of a second, and the mean velocity is $12 \times 0.25 = 3$ m.

For uniform movement with the velocity of the pressure

centre (according to § XV., we should only consider half the wing area) the wings would generate an air resistance of—

$$L = 0\cdot13 \times \frac{0\cdot06}{2} \times 3^2 = 0\cdot035 \text{ kg.}$$

In reality we find the resistance to be $0\cdot7$ kg. as proved by the fact that the bird actually flies under the observed conditions. The beating motion thus introduces a multiplying factor of 20. Expressing this in an equation, we cannot be far wrong if we take the *whole* of the surface, which with the velocity, v, of the pressure centre lying at $\frac{2}{3}$ distance produces—

$$L = 10 \times 0\cdot13Fv^2.$$

How immensely the air resistance increases for this kind of movement we can feel when we beat an ordinary fan, first rapidly to and fro, and then move it with equal but uniform velocity in the same direction. Still more pronounced does this fact become when employing light but larger surfaces; in the latter case, when the inertia of the hand is of small influence, we are positively surprised by the results, and we *feel* the air, even with small velocities, as clearly as in a storm.

§ XVII.—Economy in Energy due to Accelerated Wing Lift.

The relative durations of the upward and downward motions of the wing are of direct influence upon the energy required for flight.

They determine the magnitude of the necessary lifting air pressure and in this way the wing velocity. Both are reduced in proportion, as the greater part of the available time is spent on the downward beat, *i.e.* the quicker the bird lifts its wings for a new beat; but since work is chiefly done during the downward beat, the total amount of work is lessened when this down beat is accomplished in a shorter time.

The minimum of resistance and the minimum of absolute wing velocity would be attained if no time at all were spent on the upstroke, since in that case the necessary air pressure to be produced during the down-beat would have to be equal to the weight of the bird, G ; but then this would have to be maintained during the whole duration of flight, and the velocity of the pressure centre would enter fully into the calculation of the requisite energy—

$$\mathfrak{A} = Gv.$$

If, on the other hand, the same time is taken for the upstroke and the down-beat, the air pressure necessary to lift the bird would have to equal 2G, to be maintained during half the flight duration only.

To produce 2G the wing velocity must increase in the proportion of $\sqrt{2}$, so that the work under these conditions would equal—

$$\mathfrak{A}\sqrt{2} = 1\cdot41\mathfrak{A}.$$

Supposing the bird moved its wings twice as fast during the downstroke as during the upstroke : The lifting pressure due to former would be L, less the weight G, and would act only half as long as the weight G. The mass of the bird is, therefore, subject to two alternating and oppositely working forces, one of which—the depressing force—would act twice as long as the lifting force.

In order to keep the bird aloft, its body must execute a swinging motion, passing a given point with the same velocity, both when moving upwards and downwards. At the moment of passing through this point the active forces come into play, and the total or absolute movement will be zero if each force is capable of absorbing the velocity in one direction and to give it an opposite sign. This condition can only be fulfilled when the forces produce accelerations which are in inverse ratio to their time of persistence, or if the forces themselves are in inverse proportion to their duration.

In our case, to fulfil this condition, the lifting force, L – G must equal 2G, therefore L = 3G.

The downward velocity of the wings must, therefore, be three times as great as for L = G, namely, the theoretical case in which the whole of the available time would be employed for downstrokes. Against this we must set the fact that the velocity which requires work for its production only acts during one-third of the whole time, so that the resultant work is—

$$\mathfrak{A}3\sqrt{3} \times \tfrac{1}{3} = 1\cdot73\mathfrak{A}.$$

This demonstrates clearly that slow lifting and fast down-beat of the wings would result in a waste of energy, and would necessitate unduly strong wings on account of the greater stresses they would be subject to.

From the foregoing considerations it is easy to deduce the general law governing the effect of relative duration of upstroke and downstroke: if the duration of the down-beat be $\frac{1}{n}$ of the whole time then the work necessary for flight will be—

$$A = n\sqrt{n} \times \frac{1}{n}\mathfrak{A} = \sqrt{n}\,\mathfrak{A}.$$

Fig. 21 embodies these factors of $\mathfrak{A}$ as a curve for various

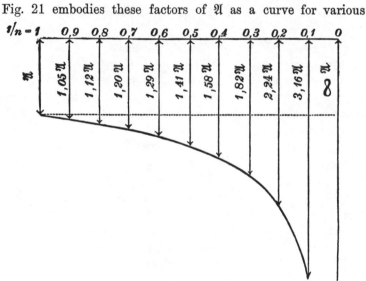

FIG. 21.

values of $\frac{1}{n}$, and shows that the conditions become the more favourable the greater the time devoted to the down-beat of the wing, i.e. the faster the wings are lifted.

There are, however, some further factors which have to be taken into account when calculating the total work required for flight and the effect of relative duration of time for up and down strokes.

In the first instances we must consider that a minimum of air resistance against the lifting of the wings can only be expected if the movement is not too rapid: also we should bear in mind that the work requisite for overcoming the mass inertia of the wings is least when the wings are lifted and beaten down with equal velocity. These two factors operate against the economy of rapid wing-lifting, but the main factor as above deduced must be accorded greater prominence, and in any case we must allow something above half time for the down-beat in order to attain the minimum of energy required for flight. A particularly suitable value of $\frac{1}{n}$ would seem to be 0·6, that is, the relative durations of up and down strokes would be as 2 : 3 and the energy 1·29$\mathfrak{A}$.

Even if this economy in energy is not very considerable, we may observe that many birds lift their wings more rapidly than they beat them downwards, and especially is this so in the case of all large birds with slowly beating wings, such as crows, who frequently accelerate the lifting of the wings whilst very slowly beating down.

§ XVIII.—The Expenditure of Energy for Flight without Locomotion (Hovering).

So long as the wings only beat up and down whilst no progress is made against the surrounding air, the foregoing calculations furnish an approximate idea of the requisite energy.

The effort required for moving the wing masses may be neglected because the wings consist at their rapidly moving end of feathers only; and the air resistance opposed to the lifting may also be neglected.

Taking the ratio of duration between up and down strokes as 0·6, the energy required for stationary flight is $A = 1·29\mathfrak{A}$ and $\mathfrak{A} = Gv$; v may be determined from equation $L = 10 \times 0·13Fv^2$, and from equation $G = 10 \times 0·13Fv^2$

$$\text{namely } v = 0·85\sqrt{\frac{G}{F}}$$

Inserting this value we obtain—

$$\mathfrak{A} = G \times 0·85\sqrt{\frac{G}{F}}$$

$$A = 1·29\mathfrak{A} = 1·1G\sqrt{\frac{G}{F}}$$

For many specimens of birds $\frac{G}{F}$ will have an approximately constant value. For many large birds $\frac{G}{F}$ approximates 9.

Example.—A bird weighs 9 kg. (Australian crane), and disposes of 1 sq. m. wing spread. $\sqrt{\frac{G}{F}}$ in this case equals 3 and

$$A = 1.1G \times 3 = 3.3G$$

For smaller birds (sparrows, etc.), $\frac{G}{F}$ frequently reaches the value of 4, and consequently $A = 2.2G$. In accordance with these equations we may conclude that "stationary flight" is far easier for small birds, because the latter have larger wings in proportion to their weights. The majority of large birds cannot fly in this manner at all, and rising in a dead calm is so very difficult that many of them have to take a forward run and hop.

Birds which are capable of maintaining themselves stationary in calm air assume a very inclined position, so that the wing-beats are not directed up and down, but partly forward and backward; pigeons especially show this peculiarity very clearly, and the wings execute such powerful rotations that it appears as if the upstroke, or rather the backstroke, would contribute towards the lifting effect.

This is necessary in order to counterbalance the normal tractive force of the wings, but it appears probable that the lifting effect is thereby strongly increased, and that for small birds who thus fly the equation may be rounded off to $A = 1.5G$. The lark is apparently more particularly fond of this kind of "stationary flight," but since it usually rises very high, and there probably meets with sufficient wind, it will require less energy than expressed by the equation.

If man would know how to utilize all the above advantages, he would require a minimum of 1.5 h.p. for stationary flight; the total weight, with an apparatus of 20 sq. m. area, would be above 80 kg., the factor $\frac{G}{F} = 4$, and the work per second consequently 120 kgm. It is, of course, out of the question that this amount of work could be furnished by muscular energy even for a short period; but this method of flight is not of immediate interest to man, and would gladly be sacrificed in favour of a method of forward flight.

§ XIX.—The Resistance to the Oblique Movement of a Plane Surface.

As soon as a bird flies forward, its wings no longer execute perpendicular movements, but describe slanting paths in the air, meeting the latter obliquely.

A wing section, ab (Fig. 22), which would arrive at a_1b_1, in the case of simple down-beat, arrives at a_2b_2 if simultaneously moved forward, and it is obvious that the air resistance and the energy

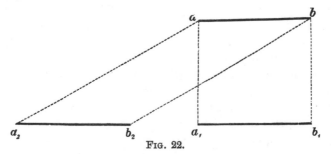

Fig. 22.

required for flight are thereby modified. Since forward flight is the most important and actual aim of the "Art of Flying," the magnitude of air resistance under these conditions is of the highest importance to us.

The formulæ to be found in technical handbooks are mostly the outcome of theoretical considerations and based on assumptions which are not verified in practice. We have already pointed out that this want of reliable data was not of much importance for the usual technical requirements; but for the practice of flight we can only use such data on air resistance, which are the result of experiments, and which take into account the imperfections of artificial wings. We cannot produce the infinitely thin and infinitely smooth wings prescribed by theory, nor does nature produce them. Hence we soon discover considerable discrepancies between practical and theoretical figures. Especially is this the case with regard to the angle between air pressure and the moved surface, which theoretically should be 90°, but which in reality considerably differs from a right angle, especially at slight inclinations, even for the thinnest and smoothest possible surfaces.

These discrepancies have already destroyed many hopes based upon the belief that forward flight would contribute towards a desirable economy in power.

The authors have been led by such assumptions to build a number of machines in order to follow up these supposed advantages.

After coming to the conclusion that rapid forward flight would increase the lifting air pressure without extra expenditure of work, we built a whole series of machines between the years 1871 and 1873 to clear these matters up. The wings of these models were moved partly by springs, partly by steam power. We succeeded in getting the models to fly freely with various speeds, but we did not succeed in establishing what we really desired: we were unable to prove that forward flight saves work, and although these experiments enriched our experience in many ways, the main result was negative as far as economy in work was concerned.

The cause of this negative result was found in wrong suppositions, and the calculations of air resistances which did not exist in practice; we were led to investigate experimentally more carefully the resistance produced by the oblique movement of surfaces, and this gave us the explanation for our negative results.

Fig. 23 shows the apparatus we employed. It enabled us to determine not only the magnitude but also the direction of the pressures produced by rotating surfaces.

The apparatus carried on a revolving vertical axis two opposite light arms with the two experimental surfaces at their extremities, which could be adjusted to any inclination. Rotation was produced by two weights, the cords of which passed over two pulleys as shown; we choose this arrangement in order to eliminate as far as possible the lateral pull on the bearings. The horizontal component of the air pressure was arrived at by reducing the propelling weight for the centres of air pressure of the surfaces, after deducting the air resistance due to the arms only, and the frictional loss which was experimentally determined beforehand. For the determination of the vertical component of the air pressure, the spindle, with all its attachments, was counterbalanced by means of a lever, at the end of which it was supported, and could move a short distance up and down, so as to demonstrate the existence of an exterior vertical force. The

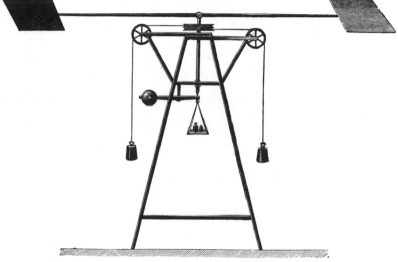

Fig. 23.

latter was then simply measured by placing weights on the scale as illustrated.

In this way we obtained for the inclined and horizontally moved surface *ab* (Fig. 24), the horizontal pressure component O*e*, and the vertical component O*f*, which gave the resultant O*g*, *i.e.* the magnitude and direction of the air pressure.

If we imagine the whole of Fig. 24 rotated through angle *a*, we obtain Fig. 25, in which ON is the perpendicular to plane *ab*. Resolving the air pressure O*g* into a vertical and a horizontal component, we find as the lifting effect for a horizontal but obliquely moved surface the force O*c*, whilst O*d* represents a restraining force in the horizontal direction. We may call O*c* the *lifting* and O*d* the *restraining* components.

The results of these investigations are embodied in Plate I., in which Fig. 1 gives the air pressure for constant direction of movement and variable inclination, whilst Fig. 2 represents the resistances as they are produced on a surface remaining parallel to itself, but moved in various directions with equal absolute velocity.

Moving a plane surface *ab*, Plate I., Fig. 1, in the direction indicated by the arrow, but under various inclinations, from $a = 0°$ to $a = 90°$, still retaining the same absolute velocity, we obtain the air resistance $c0°$, $c3°$, $c6°$, $c90°$, corresponding to the angles of inclination $0°$, $3°$, $6°$, $90°$. These values illustrate

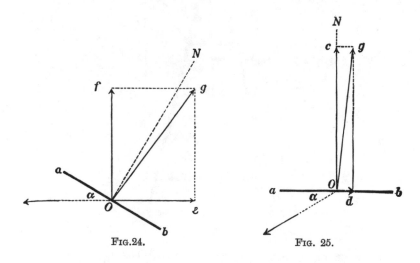

FIG. 24.   FIG. 25.

the ratio of the resistances to the normal air resistance $c90°$, calculated from equation $L = 0, 13Fv^2$, and at the same time indicate their direction.

Fig. 1 does not, however, indicate the angle between the surface and the resultant forces; this may be ascertained from Fig. 2, in which the air resistances are shown as they would be if the horizontal plane *ab* were moved in various directions ($3°$, $6°$, $9°$, etc.) with equal velocity. The angle between the vertical to the plane and the air pressure is clearly indicated.

It becomes, therefore, evident that the restraining components of the air resistance in the plane of the surface remain practically constant up to an angle of $37°$; this component also represents, to some extent, the air friction over the surface, and this friction remains almost the same if, as in Fig. 26, for acute angles, the air escapes on one side. For more obtuse angles, Fig. 27, where part of the air curls round the plane, the friction appears to be somewhat diminished, and finally in the case of normal incidence (Fig. 28) it is quite negligible, since in this case the air flows off symmetrically in all directions, and the algebraical sum of the frictions is zero.

The relation between pressure and square of velocity is not materially influenced by the friction.

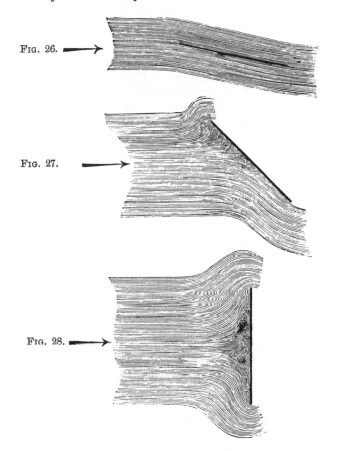

Fig. 26.

Fig. 27.

Fig. 28.

Plate VII. permits a comparison between the absolute value of the air resistance of inclined surfaces and that of vertical surfaces : the resistances of the inclined planes in relation to their angles, for constant velocity, correspond to the full line curve marked "Plane surface," which, especially for small angles, differs materially from the usually accepted sine curve. No less important are the deviations of the vertical components, because they are not much smaller.

For practical purposes the deviations of the direction of air pressure from the perpendicular are of special importance, since it is owing to them that we cannot record any economy by reason of forward flight.

It is not an easy matter to express by an equation the air pressure due to an oblique displacement, unless we neglect so many factors that the accuracy would be greatly reduced.

We have therefore to utilize the diagrams for the determination of these pressures, and for this purpose have drawn them as accurately as possible and on a large scale; they represent the mean value of the result of many experiments.

These investigations were begun in 1866, and were continued with some long interruptions until 1889. To illustrate their applicability we will mention that we constructed several experimental appliances of different dimensions, the diameter of the air path for the experimental surfaces varying between 2 m. and 7 m. The area of the surfaces, of which always two identical ones were used, varied between 0·1 and 0·5 sq. m. They were constructed of light wooden frames, covered with paper, of Press-spahn, solid wood or sheet brass; the maximum section was $\frac{1}{50}$ to $\frac{1}{80}$ of the area, and the edges were made blunt, rounded, and pointed, without, however, producing much difference, owing to the thinness of the surfaces.

The experimental velocities lay between 1 and 12 m. per second. All the experiments confirmed the law of the increase of the air resistance with the square of the velocity.

§ XX.—The Energy required in Forward Flight with Plane Wings.

If the air pressure were perpendicular to plane surfaces moved obliquely downward, rapid forward flight would result in considerable economy of energy. As shown in Fig. 29, only the small vertical component c of the velocity would have to be considered, whilst the lifting air pressure would depend upon the large absolute wing velocity, G.

The air pressure would be approximately

$$G = 0\cdot13Fv^2 \times \sin a \text{ and } v = \sqrt{\dfrac{G}{F \times 0\cdot13 \times \sin a}}$$

The work

$$G \times c = G\,.\,v\,.\sin a, \text{ or } G\,.\,c = \sqrt{\dfrac{G}{F\,.\,0\cdot13}}\,.\,\sqrt{\sin a}$$

The smaller the angle a, *i.e.* the more rapid the flight, the smaller will be $\sqrt{\sin}\ a$, and consequently the smaller the necessary work. Sufficiently rapid flight would enable us to reduce this work as much as we desire. In reality this is not strictly correct, because any existing initial velocity of the bird would soon be absorbed by the restraining component of the air resistance below the wings, even if we entirely neglect the resistance due to the bird's body.

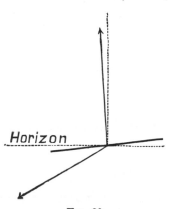

Fig. 29.

In order therefore to maintain the forward velocity of the bird, we might assume that the wings are lifted in an inclined position, a method which we included in our experiments. This would, however, produce a depressing force, which would have to be counterbalanced during the down-beat of the wings.

We may, however, imagine that the wing during the down-beat is not horizontal, but so inclined forward that the resulting force of the air pressure is exactly vertical, or slightly inclined forward in order to overcome the resistance of the bird's body (Fig. 30). We should then have an equilibrium of motion which would secure the maintenance of a certain forward velocity.

Fig. 30.

The influence of such forward flight with plane wings upon

the amount of work necessary for flight may be established as follows:—

We will call A the work required for stationary flight. Let us assume for simplicity's sake the velocity of all parts of the wing to be equal, *i.e.* that the wing remains parallel to itself in all positions, and that the distribution of the air pressure over the whole area is uniform.

Fig. 31 shows the wing section, AB, so inclined towards the horizon, that the surface which is moved, for example, at an angle of 23°, with the absolute velocity OD, produces a vertical air pressure OG. The corresponding inclination against the horizon is, according to Plate I., Figs. 1 and 2, about 6°. Now, in order to produce

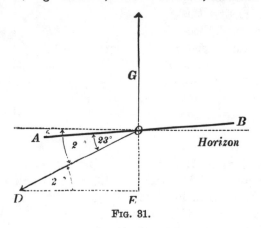

Fig. 31.

an air pressure of given value, say equal to the bird's weight G, the absolute velocity must be larger than if the surface were moved at right angles to its plane, producing the same resistance. From Plate VII. we find that, for an inclination of 23°, the air resistance is only 0·45 of that for 90°, so that the absolute velocity for this inclination would have to be multiplied by $\dfrac{1}{\sqrt{0·45}}$, *i.e.* as represented by line OD. For the work, however, only velocity OE must be considered, which equals OD × sin 29°, thus $\dfrac{1}{\sqrt{0·45}}$ × sin 29° = 0·72 of that for normal displacement.

The work being thus 0·72A, about 25 per cent. would represent the saving in work against stationary flight; the velocity of flight would then be about twice as large as the downward velocity of the wings, since ED is about twice OE. Part of this advantage is, however, again lost in overcoming the body resistance in the direction of flight.

The above condition is the most favourable, for if the wings are moved under other inclinations, *i.e.* if flying is effected more slowly or more rapidly, the result is still less favourable in comparison with the work expended. The relations to the work A are given in Plate I., Fig. 2, for a few angles, the maximum value at 23° being underlined. It is obvious that forward flight with plane wings results in but a very small economy of work, for under these conditions the theoretical minimum of energy required for human flight is only reduced from 1·5 to 1 h.p. We also know that the disability of plane surfaces in this respect is brought about by the fact that the air pressure is not directed perpendicularly to the surface when moving the latter obliquely. If, nevertheless, we have to record many attempts to calculate great advantages from complicated movements of plane wings, or even to explain the sailing flight of birds on such a basis, we are forced to the conclusion that they are based on wrong conceptions or hasty deductions, such as we unfortunately meet with all too frequently in works on flight. It looks as though there had been too much calculation and too little experiment, and that the outcome of all this was the kind of literature resulting when pure reasoning is not supported or refreshed by actual experiments.

§ XXI.—The Superiority of Natural Wings over Plane Wing Surfaces.

Since from the foregoing considerations it appears hopeless to arrive at a solution of the flight problem by means of plane wings, we must endeavour to ascertain whether the successful solution may not be brought about by wings which are not plane.

Nature demonstrates daily that flight is not at all difficult, and whenever we feel inclined to give up the idea of human flight, owing to the apparently unattainable energy required, every large bird passing us with slow deliberate wing-beats, every sailing swallow rekindles in us the thought that our calculations

E

cannot be correct; that no bird can possibly have to exert such immense energy, that somewhere there is a hidden secret which, once disclosed, would completely solve the mystery of flight.

When we observe the awkward first flying attempts of young storks, how they drop their beaks and legs and execute the most curious movements with the neck in order to re-establish their equilibrium, we conclude that such unskilled flight must be extremely easy, and we are tempted to construct a pair of wings for experimental flight.

Following the young bird's progress after the lapse of but a few days, we feel encouraged to emulate its example.

After a very short while the young stork, before his departure south, soars without a single wing-beat by the side of its parents in the blue of the ether. Does not this demonstrate the importance of having the proper wing shape? Once we know this, everything else becomes natural. If we further remember that the majority of birds are endowed with the power of flight, not sparingly, but to a profligate extent, the hope almost becomes a conviction that artificial human flight, if properly executed and with properly shaped wings, may be possible. That birds often possess a surplus of flight power is evident from the fact that some of them are able to carry their prey, which may be of considerable weight. The pigeon, which is carried off by the hawk, weighs nearly half as much as the latter, and certainly does not contribute to the lifting effort, since its wings are pressed together by the talons of its captor. Of course, the exertion necessary for such transport is very obvious; still the hawk is able to fly long distances thus burdened, and could surely do even better if it were not for the desperate attempts of the frightened victim to regain its liberty, and for the fact that the nearly doubled area presented by the two birds prevents rapid flight. The size of the wings of birds is generally very liberal, and this is proved by their ability to fly with largely reduced wings. The want of a few large feathers does not generally result in any visible difference in its flying powers.

It may be well here to recall to mind that the tail area of birds is of very small importance as compared with the wing effect, because even after the loss of *all* tail feathers flight is barely impaired. This applies not only to the lifting power, but also to horizontal steering; a sparrow, after losing its tail, flies as surely through a fence as its fellow birds. The tail appears to be, however, of considerable importance for vertical steering, a fact which is already evinced by the horizontal disposition of the tail-feathers as compared with the vertical position of a fish's tail.

It is also worth while remembering that birds with long necks are endowed with short tails, and *vice versâ*. The long neck is well adapted for shifting the centre of gravity, and by its aid the inclination of the bird may be rapidly altered. The long tail is well fitted to replace the long neck, not for the purpose of shifting the centre of gravity, but by creating a lifting or depressing air pressure exactly like a horizontal rudder.

If, notwithstanding, the tail can be dispensed with, it is because the bird possesses still another most effective means of lifting or lowering its front portion. It has only to shift the pressure centre forward, by pushing forward its wings, in order to be instantly lifted in front, or to draw the wings backward in order to incline forward; this latter movement is made use of by birds of prey when dropping upon their victims from above.

The author has carried out experiments with a view of determining the necessary wing area for pigeons. By clipping the wings the limit is soon reached, but by tying several feathers together we can go a great deal further.

Fig. 32 illustrates the limits in this respect at which the pigeon is still able to fly rapidly and high for a prolonged period.

FIG. 32.

To show still more clearly what little energy is evidently required for flight we will cite an example from the realm of flying insects, though the comparison seems somewhat far-fetched. We may mention the ordinary house-fly, which during the autumn is barely able to move, is yet quite able to fly. It is true that the smaller creatures have larger wing areas in comparison with their weight, and that in consequence flight is made much easier for insects. 1 kg. weight of sparrows shows only 0·25 sq. m. wing area, whilst for 1 kg. weight of libellæ the wing area is 2·5 sq. m.

It is for this reason that we should not take the insect world as our model for flying, but, on the contrary, we must study the large flyers, for whom the ratio between wing area and weight approaches as nearly as possible those conditions which are necessary for human flight.

Our attention has been drawn to the shape of the wings, and we all know that birds' wings are not plane, but somewhat curved.

The question therefore arises whether this fact is capable of explaining the small amount of energy necessary for natural flight, and in how far wings other than planes are of assistance in reducing the work of flying. Theoretical predictions do not seem to be of much use in this respect, except by referring us back again and again to nature and to the exact imitation of a bird's wing.

§ XXII.—The Determination of the Wing Shapes.

The curvature of a bird's wing seems to be too small to account for the remarkable difference in the effect. This also was our idea when, in the year 1888, during the summer holidays, we erected an experimental apparatus (in a large Berlin gymnasium) and fitted it with various curved surfaces in order to discover, if possible, still better shapes of wing than those designed by nature Such an arrangement we have already described and illustrated in Fig. 23. It enables us to determine the magnitude and direction of the air pressure on various surfaces, the latter being moved with various velocities and at various angles.

The surfaces were made of flexible material, so that they could be given any desired shape. We endeavoured to establish comparisons between the effects of different wing shapes with a view of ascertaining their suitability for aviation. It was our aim to discover that shape which showed the greatest economy in the

work required for flight. This work, as we know, is the product
of force and velocity, and any reduction of it means the reduction
of either or both factors. The force, having to be always at least
equal to the weight to be lifted, cannot be reduced, and our
attention must therefore be directed to the relative velocity, *i.e.*
upon the velocity of the wings relative to the body of the bird,
especially the vertical speed component of the pressure centre.
The question arises: are there any shapes which, when used as
wings and moved for forward flight, produce greater lifting and
less retarding effect than would the plane surface under identical
conditions? *We must find a shape which, when moved in a certain
position, namely, at a very acute angle with the horizon, produces
a maximum of weight-lifting component and a minimum of retarding or drifting component of the air pressure.*

The value of the wing shape is measured by the *magnitude* and
purity of *lifting effect* produced by moving the wing simultaneously
slowly downward and rapidly forward.

§ XXIII.—The most favourable Wing Section.

The wings with which we experimented had the sections shown
in Fig. 33; their other shape will be considered later on. The

Fig. 33.

experiment showed that of all these surfaces the simple and very
slightly curved surface (analogous to the bird's wing) possessed
pre-eminently those qualities which we considered essential for
economy in flight.

A slightly curved surface, with the section shown in Fig. 34,
when moved in the direction of the arrow, produces an air pressure,
oa, having a considerable lifting component, *ob*, and only a small
drifting component, *oc*; for certain inclinations there is no drift at
all, and, contrary to all expectations, this component assumes
such a direction to the surface as to produce a propelling effect.

Since it is probable that the whole secret of flight is to be found in the properties of such slightly curved surfaces, we must investigate them more minutely later on. But first we shall compare the general behaviour of flat and curved surfaces as regards the energy required for flight. This will show us the advantage of curved surfaces and the necessity of entirely abandoning plane surfaces for flight.

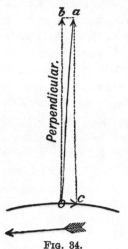

Fig. 34.

§ XXIV. — The Advantages of Curved Wings over Plane Surfaces.

In order to arrive at a comparison between the air pressure on plane and that on curved surfaces, we represent in Figs. 35 and 36 two surfaces, *ab* and *cd*, in section, of equal area, making the same angle of about 15° with the horizon, provided we consider

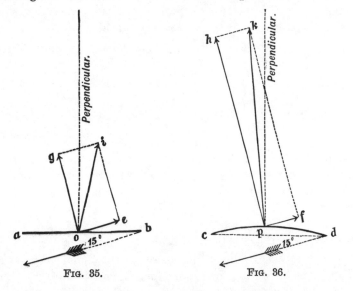

Fig. 35.   Fig. 36.

the chord *cd* for the curved surface as its direction. On moving these surfaces horizontally with equal velocity through still air by means of the whirling arrangement shown in Fig. 23, and investigating the resulting air pressure, we obtain the horizontal components *oe* and *pf*, and the vertical components *og* and *ph*, which have been drawn to scale in the figures from the experiments.

Constructing from these components the resultants *oi* and *pk* gives us the absolute magnitude and direction of the air pressure for both surfaces.

To fully grasp the importance of this difference for the requisite flight energy, let us assume the two surfaces to be placed horizontally, and their velocity directed downwards at an angle of 15°; the parallelograms of forces are then shown in Figs. 37 and 38.

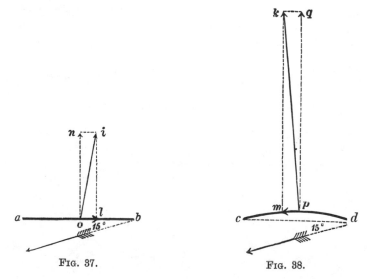

FIG. 37. FIG. 38.

Employing the surfaces *ab* and *cd* as wings in this position, with the velocity *v*, we are at once struck by the fact that the curved surface exerts a greater lifting power for a given speed, so that it may be possible to move such a surface more slowly than a plane surface whilst yet attaining the same lifting effect, and thereby economizing " work."

Of still greater importance, however, is the more favourable direction of the resulting air pressure in the case of a curved surface. The retarding component, *ol*, of the plane surface is replaced by a *pushing* component, *pm*, so that the real obstacle to the attainment of power economy in forward flight is removed when using a curved surface, which possesses all those advantages so long and unsuccessfully searched for in the case of plane wings.

Before we occupy ourselves more closely with the resulting power economy, we propose considering theoretically the causes of these phenomena, which are of equal importance for the bird-world and for aviation.

§ XXV.—The Difference between Plane and Curved Surfaces as regards Air Resistance.

Experiment enables us to determine the actual degree of superiority of curved over plane wings, but in view of the importance of this matter we must obtain a perfect conception of the nature of this phenomenon. In Fig. 39, we imagine two surfaces of

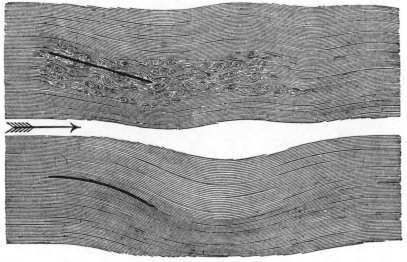

FIG. 39.

equal area, one plane, the other slightly curved, and placed in a uniform horizontal current of air. The phenomena of air resistance remain substantially the same, whether the surfaces are moved in still air or whether the air moves with the same velocity against the surfaces. In the present instance we assume the air to be moving, in order to be able to indicate the paths of the air particles and to obtain a clear idea of the prevailing conditions. Both surfaces are again supposed to have the same inclination and area, and we take the chord of the curve to represent the direction of the corresponding surface. It is at once obvious that the conditions obtaining in the air must be different for both cases, and that the resulting air pressure must vary, even though the curvature of the wing is very slight. Although the picture may not be exactly in accordance with reality (the streams being invisible), it will suffice for the necessary considerations if the characteristic differences approximate at least to fact. The air which streams past the surfaces is in both cases subject to a downward acceleration, since the air, striking below the surface, must pass underneath, and the air streaming past the upper face, must fill the space above; the exact mode in which this takes place is, however, different in the two cases.

The deviation downward of the air stream takes place generally at the leading edge of the plane surface, and rather suddenly, giving rise to shocks and to the formation of eddies. This fact alone, according to the general principles of dynamics, produces a diminution of the desired effect, because the production of accidental, secondary effects, represents some loss so far as the main effect is concerned. This main effect, however, should be a reaction pressure on the surface, directed as nearly vertically upward as possible, and as large as possible, and this we can only expect if the surface imparts to the air the most perfect acceleration directed as nearly as possible in a downward direction. All eddies, however, consist of circular movements, *i.e.* accelerations in every direction, of which but a small proportion is utilized for lifting effects, whilst the rest represents losses. As indicated by the figure, the air stream impinging on the plane will be disturbed, and the eddies and irregular movements in the air will persist for some time in the wake of the plane, and the momentum of these eddies will only gradually become absorbed by friction. A plane surface will mainly exert its acceleration upon the air at the leading edge, since the air particles, after contact with that edge, must essentially assume the path given by the direction of the plane. We may, therefore, say that the centre of pressure in the case of such an obliquely travelling plane, is not in the geometrical centre of the plane, but nearer the leading edge; so that the distribution of the air pressure is not uniform, but increases towards the leading edge.

A considerable portion of the plane surface will therefore allow the air to stream past without appreciable effect, and the leading part of the surface can only act detrimentally in view of the unavoidable shock.

Totally different are the phenomena in the case of a *curved* surface.

The air stream on meeting such a surface is quite gradually deflected from its horizontal direction, and turned downward, acquiring its downward velocity gradually, and practically without shock.

It is evident that only a slightly and smoothly curved surface, especially one with the tangent of the leading edge as nearly as possible in the wind direction, can allow the air to stream past it without producing eddies, and then leave the trailing edge with a velocity which corresponds in direction with the tangent of this edge. Theoretically, only a parabolic curve would impart a uniform acceleration to the air; but such shallow parabolas do not differ much from circular arcs, yet it is possible to prove the parabolic section of a bird's wing.

The downward component of the momentum of the air particles, after leaving the surface, determines the upward pressure on this surface. The air leaves a curved surface in an orderly mass, and owing to its momentum will of course pass downward still further: the result thereof is a vertical air movement of far greater extent than the actual projection of the surface in the wind direction.

This is the main difference between the two surfaces, and this accounts also for the important difference in the resulting air pressure. Whilst the plane gives rise to many eddies with lesser vertical components, a proper curve produces a vertical oscillatory motion in the air, of which the vertical component is very large. *The lifting effect is in direct proportion to the perfection of this wave motion, and the purer the vertical oscillation, the more perfect is the pure lifting effect upon the curved surface according to the principle of action and reaction.*

We must therefore endeavour to avoid, as far as possible, any formation of eddies and occurrence of shocks during forward flight, a condition for which the plane wing is utterly unsuitable.

We may, speaking generally, conclude that we have treated the air which is to sustain us in flight too roughly. The air which is to carry us with a minimum of mechanical work on our part should not be torn, crushed, or broken by plane surfaces, but should be curved and softly deflected from its direction by means of suitably curved surfaces. The wind which passes underneath the wings must not meet plane surfaces but surfaces to which it can cling, so as to gradually, though as completely as possible, yield its momentum, converting it into lifting effect with a minimum of drift.

If the view be correct that possibly in the avoidance of eddies lies the principle which may some day enable us to actually fly, then we may investigate the secrets of air resistance almost with closed eyes. Even the ear tells us whether we deal with pure wave motion or with wasteful eddies. We therefore prefer those surfaces which, even at considerable velocities in air, do not produce noise to those which produce a rushing noise under the same conditions; and even applying this test, the wings of birds come out best.

There still exist some other points of difference between curved and flat surfaces. A curved surface deflects the air in an arc, though it may not be quite as smoothly as indicated in Fig. 39. This curvilinear motion of the air particles gives rise to a definite centrifugal force with which the particles below the surface press against the latter, whilst those above exert a suction effect so that both produce a lifting effect. If we ascribe the actually determined pressure to centrifugal force alone we obtain a result which is in accord with our assumption. The centrifugal force also increases with the square of the velocity.

Centrifugal force does not come into question when dealing with plane surfaces, which is another reason for the great contrast between the pressures obtained for the two types of surfaces.

From the more forward inclination of the direction of the air pressure on curved surfaces we may conclude that the distribution of the pressure is somewhat irregular, greater pressure being exerted on those portions the perpendiculars to which are set

Wind
FIG. 40.

more square to the wind direction, somewhat as shown in Fig. 40.

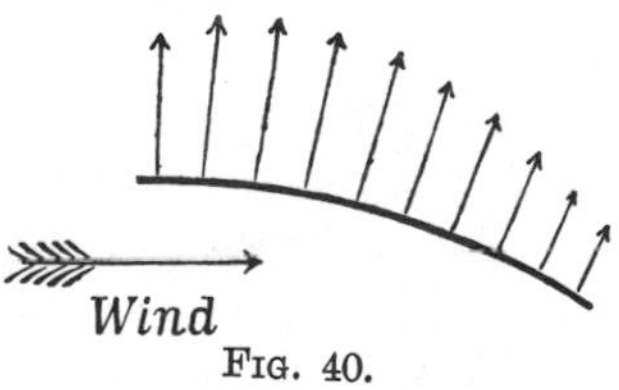

§ XXVI.—The Influence of Wing Outlines.

The analysis of air resistance by sound, mentioned in the last section, may also be applied to the investigation of the influence of the outline of the surfaces under test; indeed, it was this method which induced us to devote our attention to this factor.

It is evidently not immaterial whether an obliquely placed, rectangular surface is pushed through the air lengthways or sideways. Though the two surfaces, A and B, shown in plan (Fig. 41) are of equal area, have equal inclinations and equal velocity, there is a difference between both as regards the air resistance, which points to the formation of eddies to a greater extent on A

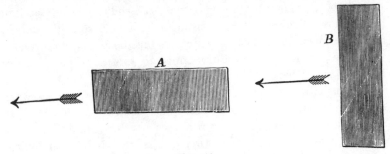

Fig. 41.

than on B, *i.e.* the former will emit a stronger rushing sound. This is in perfect accord with the wave theory set forth in the last section. Surface B, though smooth, produces an imperfect air wave of a given width; there will be eddies at the short sides, resulting in losses and causing sound; part of the air will pass by without doing work. This minor disadvantage arising from the shortness of the side edges will, however, become of great magnitude for the surface A, since the side edges form the greater portion of the whole outline.

The air which passes below the short leading edge probably does not reach the trailing edge at all, but escapes laterally, and there will be less chance of a perfect wave production than in the case of B.

When moving plane surfaces vertically to their extension in air, only the area and not the shape of the surface entered into the calculation of the resulting air pressure; when moving such planes, however, obliquely, we find that the shape largely influences this pressure.

In the case of curved surfaces, which may otherwise conform to every condition of producing favourable air pressures, if the sides are cut square, as shown in Fig. 42, the formation of eddies at the sides cannot be avoided, since we cannot assume the resulting air wave to be divided from the still or rectilinearly moving air by a sharp line.

To avoid this we must point the outline of the surface, as shown in Fig. 43, so as to reduce the wave motion laterally and gradually.

Nature likewise confirms this reasoning; all birds' wings, besides being cambered, terminate in points, and those the outlines of which are not so shaped are resolved into several smaller points (pinions), a proof that in this case the sustaining air wave is split up into a number of smaller waves: another way of affecting the gradual lateral blending off of the main wave into the surrounding air. That the outline of the wings, whilst conforming to these conditions, may be extremely varied is shown by the types of wings collected in Fig. 44. Some birds, such as the stork, show resolved wing termination; others, such as the swallow, the gull, and even the bat, have closed wings.

§ XXVII.—The Determination of the Air Pressure on Birds' Wing Surfaces.

From the above considerations we are justified in stating that if we call the laws of air resistance the general foundations of aviation, the knowledge of the laws relating to the air resistance of curved surfaces, similar to birds' wings, actually forms the basis for every effective research into actual flight.

It is just as thankless to calculate the purely theoretical value of pressures on curved surfaces as it was for plane surfaces. It is true that we may obtain a number of interesting theoretical facts, and indeed the dynamics of curved surfaces in air are more amenable to correct theoretical treatment than those of planes obliquely moved; but it is obvious that in practice things are not

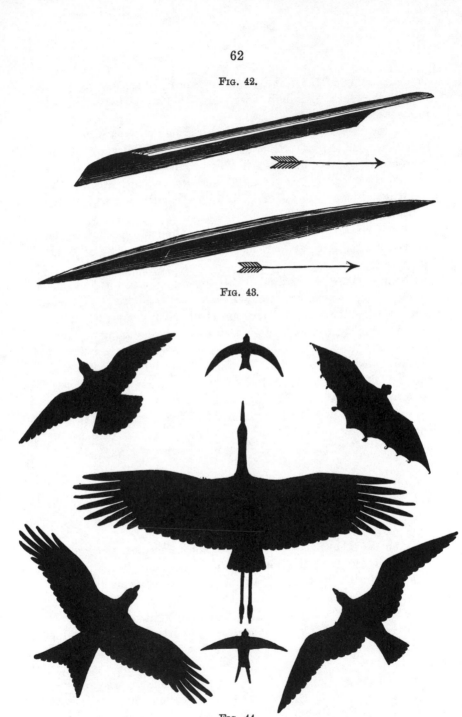

Fig. 42.

Fig. 43.

Fig. 44.

so simple as Fig. 39 represents, a picture which was only intended to serve for an illustration of the typical differences between curved and plane surfaces.

For the determination of air pressures on curved wings under different inclinations, we must have recourse to experiment; only actual measurements of forces can give us useful figures for the explanation of birdflight and for aviation.

We may either move the experimental wing in still air, or we may cause air to impinge on the wing.

In the former case we are limited to a circular movement of the wing, and have to employ an apparatus similar to Fig. 23.

Rectilinear movement of the surfaces would necessitate mechanism with greater secondary resistances, and consequently would introduce greater sources of error. On the other hand, the whirling machine does not allow us to investigate rectilinear motion; after half a rotation, the wing under test enters a region of disturbed air, thus introducing errors. Both disadvantages decrease as the diameter of the circular path increases, so that such machines ought to be made as large as possible.

The second method—that of exposing the test surface to the wind—though giving the effect of rectilinear motion, suffers from this defect: the strength of the wind varies almost every second, and it is extremely difficult to seize those moments during which the anemometer indicates the proper velocity. It is, therefore, necessary to determine by means of very numerous experiments good average values.

We have repeatedly employed both methods of measurement because we were impressed with the importance of obtaining the most accurate knowledge of the air pressures on curved surfaces, and because we desired to check the various methods one with the other, as we had no knowledge of similar experiments made by others which would have permitted us to check our own results.

There exists a simple method of determining the actual curvature of a bird's wing as it must be when the bird rests on the air. A dead wing, or an inactive live wing, appears more curved than it really is during flight, since the feathers, which are more curved in the inactive state, will be somewhat flattened by the air pressure from below when in flight.

The same effect may also be attained by fixing a fresh bird's wing in the reverse position at the shoulder end and loading it with sand, weighing fully as much as half of the bird's weight (Fig. 45).

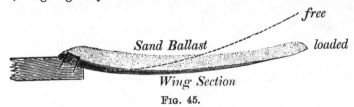

free

Sand Ballast .... *loaded*

Wing Section

Fig. 45.

In the case of good flyers, such as sea birds, the curvature is slight, height h, in Fig. 46, amounting to $\frac{1}{12}$ to $\frac{1}{15}$ of the wing

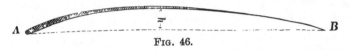

A .... B

Fig. 46.

length AB; indifferent flyers and running birds have strongly curved wings.

§ XXVIII.—The Air Pressure on Birds' Wings determined on Rotating Surfaces.

The following results were obtained by attaching wing-like surfaces to a large rotating or whirling machine, having a diameter of 7 metres, the test surfaces being arranged at a height of $4\frac{1}{2}$ metres above ground. As the machine was erected in the open, experiments were only carried out during perfect calms; buildings and trees were sufficiently far away not to exert any disturbing influence upon the test surfaces. A number of high and densely foliated trees surrounding the test ground at some distance afforded, however, certain protection, so that experiments were possible during many summer evenings. The area of both test surfaces amounted in every case to $\frac{1}{2}$ sq. m. each, so that the determined total pressure referred to an area of 1 sq. m. The outline of the test surfaces was that shown in Fig. 47, with a width of 0·4 m. and a length of 1·8 m.; the test objects or surfaces, as well as their moulding, were produced in a variety of ways.

At first sight, it seems as though the air pressure would show most favourably if the surfaces were taken as thin as possible, and we therefore made our test surfaces of thin sheet-metal. But

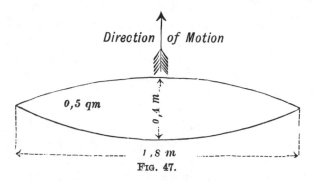

Fig. 47.

the rigidity of such test objects, even if strongly curved, when made of ½ mm. thick, hard, brass sheet, was found to be insufficient for the purpose of these experiments, and we had to bind the outline with 4 mm. steel wire in order to attain the requisite stability. Fig. 48 represents the section (scale 1 : 5). This form

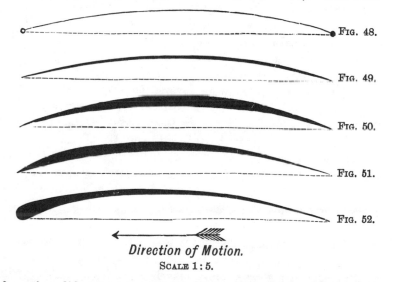

Direction of Motion.
SCALE 1 : 5.

of section did not possess such favourable air pressure features as the following, since the advantage of using thin sheets was destroyed by the disturbing influence of the wire edges.

The sections shown in Figs. 49 to 52 produced almost

F

equally good results. No appreciable differences could be found whether the section was of the same thickness all over (about 6 mm.), as in Fig. 49, or with a thickening in the middle (Fig. 50), or whether this thickening lay more towards the leading edge (Fig. 51). With a width of 400 mm. it was possible to increase these gradual thickenings to 16 mm., or $\frac{1}{25}$ of the width, without adversely affecting the air pressure. Contrary to expectation, no disadvantage accrued even from placing the thickening right at the leading edge, as in Fig. 52; it even appeared as though this shape possessed specially favourable properties as regards air pressure, namely, great lifting and very little retarding pressure, more particularly so when moving under very acute angles, but only when the thickening was in front and not at the trailing edge. Generally speaking, there was no great difference between the sections 48–52, and our results refer equally to all these sections. The test objects (Figs. 49–52) were made of wood; we obtained the very slight curvatures by gumming paper to one face only of thin boards, which caused them to warp. The stronger curvatures were worked out of the massive wood. Where the width of the curvatures decreased, the section was correspondingly altered so as to always maintain its relative proportions. Section 52 was constructed by taking for the leading edge a stout willow cane, tapering towards both ends, and joining to this cane curved cross ribs, which were covered on both sides with oiled paper, and thus formed smooth surfaces both above and below. The wing of a bird shows a similar section at its upper part where the leading edge is thickened through the bones.

As proved by experiment, this thickening in no way interferes with the flight so long as it decreases towards the wing tips. Our various constructions proved to us the unsuitability of metals for making wings, and that the wings of the future will in all probability consist of willow cane covered with a light material. Bamboo, likewise, does not lend itself so perfectly to wing forms as the naturally tapering willow wood, which can be worked to a certain extent, and may be bent to any degree whilst moist, and which also combines great toughness with extreme lightness.

Willow wood only breaks at a strain of 8 kg. per sq. mm., and may be permanently strained with 2–3 kg. with a good factor of safety ; moreover, it is the lightest of all woods, its specific weight being 0·33. Aluminium is eight times as heavy, and has barely four times the strength. It is stated that aluminium, in the shape of conical tubes, lends itself to specially light constructions, but willow canes may easily be hollowed out, because a centre-bit with blunt centerguide will not run out but be guided by the pith. By employing drills of varying thickness the bore may be reduced towards the ends. The above-described test surfaces were made in various curvatures, and tried for air pressure. The amount of curvature is measured by the camber below the surface, and the area by the projection of the surface. As in the case of experiments with plane surfaces, the two components of the air resistance were measured separately, and then determined as to magnitude and direction.

For a slight curvature of $\frac{1}{40}$ width, *i.e.* for 1 cm. depth, we obtained diagram on Plate II. Fig. 1, Plate II., represents the magnitude and direction of the air pressures which result from moving the surface with section *ab* under different inclinations in the direction of the arrow. The maximum air pressure is produced when the surface is in position FG, *i.e.* for an inclination of 90°, and it is plotted in the curve from C to the right, along line C 90°. For position *de*, and inclination 20°, the absolute velocity remaining equal, the resulting air pressure is shown as C 20°. The air pressures for 3°, 6°, 9°, etc., are shown as C 3°, C 6°, C 9°, etc. Even for position *ab* and inclination 0°, we still obtain a lifting air pressure C 0.

As slight curvatures are without effect upon the air pressure C 90°, it is always to be calculated according to formula: $L = 0\cdot13Fv^2$.

Diagram on Plate VII. shows the relations for equal velocity, but varying inclination of the air pressure to the normal air resistance, and they may be read off directly from the lowest small dotted line; the direction of the pressures may be seen from Plate II.

We are therefore able to determine the amount and direction of the air pressure on a very slightly curved surface ($\frac{1}{40}$ width), for every inclination between 0° and 90°.

For greater curvatures ($\frac{1}{25}$ width) we obtain Fig. 1 on Plate III., and in Plate VII., the second, small dotted line.

Pressure for C 90° again equals that in Plate I. and Plate II., but the other pressures have appreciably increased, and their directions are somewhat different; especially noticeable is this increase for 0°, and this lifting effect only ceases when the leading edge is at a lower level than the trailing edge, *i.e.* for an inclination of − 4°.

Still more surprising effects are obtained if the curvature is increased to $\frac{1}{12}$ width; these are recorded in Fig. 1, Plate IV. For C 90° we again have L = 0·13Fv^2, that is to say, the same as though the surface were plane. But at other inclinations the air pressures differ most materially from those of a plane surface under similar inclinations and velocities. For the sake of easy comparison, the pressures for a plane surface are shown dotted in Plate IV., Fig. 1, and the advantages of a curved surface over a plane, for flight purposes, are clearly shown.

Plate VII. shows quite plainly that the curving of a surface for acute angles up to 20° practically doubles the air pressure, but Plate IV. permits us to recognize the more favourable direction of these air pressures, and their suitability for forward flight.

If we increase the curvatures beyond $\frac{1}{12}$ width, the favourable qualities gradually disappear again; the air pressure shows a smaller lifting component and a more unfavourable direction.

We therefore consider a curvature of $\frac{1}{12}$ width as the best curvature, at least for the velocities obtaining in our experiments, *i.e.* up to 12 m. per second.

It is possible that at still higher velocities a somewhat lesser curvature will give the most favourable conditions; there were such indications.

§ XXIX.—Comparison of the Direction of the Air Pressures.

It is possible to draw for the curved surfaces diagrams which are similar to those drawn in Plate I. for the plane surface, and which give an idea of the direction of the air pressures.

Corresponding with Fig. 2, Plate I., we may draw up Fig. 2 on Plates II., III., IV., assuming the test surface to be placed horizontally, and moved obliquely downward in various directions, but with equal absolute velocity.

These figures may be obtained from Fig. 1 by rotating each respective line of air pressure until the corresponding surface is horizontal. Each line must thus be swung round point C through an angle corresponding to the number of degrees marked at its end. Under these conditions the characteristic difference of curved surfaces against planes appears still more striking; not only does the direction of the air pressures closely approach that of the perpendicular to the surface, but for certain angles it actually passes beyond it to the other side, converting the usual restraining component into a propelling component.

Curved surfaces, when placed horizontally, and moved downward under certain angles, have therefore the tendency to *automatically* increase the horizontal velocity. This also is an explanation of the unstable behaviour of slightly curved parachutes. Light bodies, consisting of shallow curves, when falling in air, describe peculiar paths, and every piece of blotting paper which drops from our desk reminds us, by its erratic movements of those properties of curved surfaces.

According to the diagrams, Fig. 2, on Plates II., III., and IV., the propelling component is a maximum when the surfaces are approximately moved in the direction of the tangent to the leading edge; in this case the wave production is probably most perfect, and the view expressed in § XXV, Fig 39, is perfectly corroborated.

It follows that for specially rapid flight a slightly curved wing is best suited, since the leading tangent indicates an absolute path corresponding to very great velocity.

§ XXX.—The Work necessary for Forward Flight with Curved Wings.

From the advantages of curved surfaces demonstrated in the previous sections, it becomes evident that the amount of mechanical work required for forward flight with curved wings must be considerably reduced.

It is possible to again calculate, as in § XX., the relation between the work necessary for different degrees of forward flight and that necessary for stationary flight: in both cases assuming curved wings. Denoting the latter work again by A, we obtain for forward flight from Fig. 2, on Plates II., III., and IV., the proportions for the work when the wings are fully spread and beating downward under the angles shown.

The minimum for the best curvature is found at 15°, and amounts to 0·23A (this corresponds to a flight velocity of four times the downward velocity of the wings, assuming the latter to be moved parallel to themselves), therefore less than a $\frac{1}{4}$ of the work necessary for hovering flight is required.

Whilst this saving of energy amounts for plane wings to about 25 per cent., according to § XX. and Plate I., Fig. 2, the curved surface shows a saving of 75 per cent. It is questionable whether forward flight gives the same advantages of the wing-beat motion as does hovering flight; to a certain extent it probably does. If it did so nearly to the same extent, the work necessary for flight would be reduced to $\frac{1}{4}$ of that necessary for stationary flight, provided the forward velocity is four times the velocity with which the wings are beaten down, and that the camber of the wings is $\frac{1}{12}$ of the width. According to § XVIII., the energy necessary to maintain man in stationary flight with very large, light wings, was found to be 1·5 h.p.; for man flying forward with suitably curved wings, this energy under the most favourable but probably unattainable conditions, would be $1·5 \times \frac{1}{4} = 0·4$ h.p., but even this amount could only be exerted by man for a short time. We have thus to discover still more favourable phenomena before it becomes possible to maintain ourselves in the air by our own muscular efforts.

The advantages thus far secured by means of a proper wing-shape are unmistakable; we will, however, not dwell any longer upon the subject since we shall see that the assumptions so far made for the air conditions cannot be so simply applied to the practice of flight.

For our last calculations we have employed the values of air pressures obtained in still air by means of the whirling machine. Later on we shall consider similar investigations made in the wind and which give much better results; but before doing so we have to make a few general remarks concerning the behaviour of the birds in the wind.

§ XXXI.—Birds and Wind.

It is even more correct to call the wind (rather than the air) the proper element of birds. We have already seen that wind facilitates the rising of birds, and that many birds in the absence of such wind have to create a relative air motion before they are able to rise. We also observe that the flying movements of birds in a wind are different to those executed in calm air. The fluttering motions during a calm change to slower and regular motions in the wind and with many birds develop into true sailing flight.

Although the wind obviously permits the birds to economize in energy during flight, by facilitating their flotation, as we will prove later on, the opinion that birds show a special preference for flying against the wind is erroneous, and can only be affirmed as regards their rising. Once in the air, those factors which facilitated the rising no longer apply; the bird is then able to reach the necessary relative velocity against the surrounding air, even if flying with the wind, provided his own speed exceeds that of the wind.

The important factor is the velocity of the bird relative to the air, and this relatively moving air always meets the bird from the front, producing the sensation of a head wind. The whole design of the bird's plumage in general and the construction of his wings in particular, with regard to the super-imposition of the feathers, make it appear improbable that the wind should ever strike a bird in flight from the rear. For this same reason we must reject as illogical all those explanations of the "circling" of birds, according to which the bird, when flying against the wind, allows the latter to strike the underside of the wings, and then, when flying with the wind, allows it to press from behind below the wings. The absolute velocities of the birds when flying against and with the wind differ on the average by the double wind velocity, since the latter is in one case deducted from, and in the other case added to, the relative motion between bird and wind.

A velocity of 10 m. for the bird, and of 6 m. for the wind, are normal values; their difference, viz. 4 m., would be the actual velocity of the bird when flying against the wind, and their sum viz. 16 m., the velocity when flying with the wind ; with greater wind velocities, these differences become still more pronounced.

We may assume that the birds endeavour to equalize these differences in their absolute velocities since they also try to fly as fast as possible against the wind, and that in reality the differences are not quite so great, yet they cannot be reduced below a certain limit, and on the average we may say that flying against the wind occupies twice as long as flying with the wind. This may account for the notion that birds find flight against the wind easy, since when observing birds it appears as though they were flying more frequently against the wind, because this occupies a longer time.

If birds fly in directions which enclose an angle with the wind direction, they experience the sensation of a wind in a direction which is the resultant of the wind direction and that of their own absolute flight.

If, for instance, the bird wishes to fly in the direction of *ob* (Fig. 53), with a prevailing wind *oa*, he will place his axis in the direction

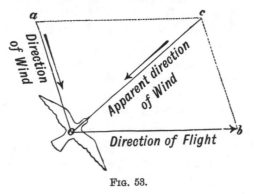

FIG. 53.

oc, since he feels the wind blowing from *c* with the velocity *co*.

Sometimes the force of the wind is so great that the smaller birds cannot make headway against it. Our investigations showed us, for instance, that for a wind velocity of 12 m., measured at a distance of 3 m. above ground, crows and rooks, at an altitude of about 50 m., battled in vain against the wind. We estimated the wind velocity at this altitude at 15–18 m. With still smaller birds (except swallows) this limit would probably be attained earlier.

All sea birds, however, even the smallest species, are an exception, and seem to be able to fly in the heaviest gale.

The great flight artists of the high seas, especially the albatross, show even such a predilection for the wind that they entirely avoid stretches of sea with frequent calms, and chiefly inhabit such latitudes and seas in which the wind is regular and strong. The albatross in particular knows how to master a gale with his long, narrow, almost swordlike wings; his heavy body sails on the hurricane by means of his slender flight apparatus, only slightly turning and shifting the wings, and arriving wherever he lists, either with the gale or against it, the only noticeable difference between both cases being the speed attained.

It is possible to closely, and for a long time, study the albatross, since in certain latitudes, for instance at the Cape, it is a constant follower of the steamer and a favourite of the seamen, who admire its majestic movements with which it plays round the ship.

My brother frequently noticed with what surprising ease the albatross passed in an inclined position through gaps in the rigging which barely gave room for his spread. Imagine what skill is required to combine the velocity of the gale, the speed of the great Australian liners, and the inherent speed of the bird so as to enable the latter to accomplish such acrobatic feats. These latter, however, are not the real aim of the bird. Its greenish eyes clearly express the main object, namely, to search for tit-bits such as the sea cannot offer; so these birds are simultaneously able to execute a fourth movement, *i.e.* to snatch, and mutually hunt each other for any remnants thrown to them from aboard.

Very remarkable and characteristic also is the rising of the floating sea birds in a strong wind. The pure lifting effect of the wind is still more clearly to be seen than when the bird is aloft.

I have often observed at close quarters how the gulls, with their wings spread, but motionless, were lifted vertically from the sea and continued their flight without beating the wings, but it was only when the wind had an estimated velocity of at least 10 m.

All these observations naturally force us to pay attention to the wind, when determining air pressure. Such experiments are more difficult than those made by means of a whirling machine, but obviously we shall be able to arrive in this way much nearer the actual relations existing between birds and wind, then by deducting these from experiments in calm air. We shall also be able to ascertain whether the wind possesses properties which make for economy in energy during flight. At any rate, it is best to expose for this purpose test surfaces similar to birds' wings to the wind, and to measure the resulting air pressures.

§ XXXII.—The Air Pressure on a Bird's Wing measured in the Wind.

For this experiment we may employ apparatus such as illustrated in Figs. 54 and 55.

Fig. 54 shows the adjustment for determining horizontal

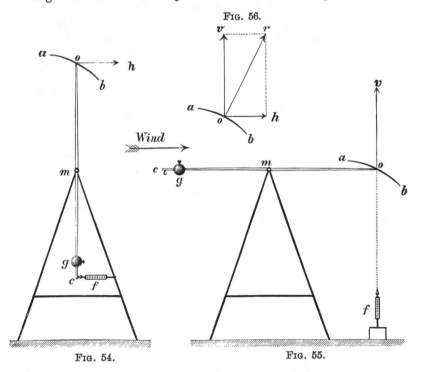

FIG. 56.

FIG. 54.   FIG. 55.

wind pressures, and Fig. 55 that for determining the vertical lifts due to the wind. In both cases the test surface, which has the section *ab*, is fitted to a double lever *oc*, and this lever is balanced by means of a counter-weight *g*, so that in calm air the lever with the test surface remains in any position. If the wind presses on the surface *ab*, as in Fig. 54, it endeavours to turn the lever around the fulcrum *m*, with the force *oh*, and if the two levers are equal, we can read this force directly by means of a small spring balance fixed to the end *c*. This force, *oh*, is the horizontal component of the wind pressure acting upon the surface. In a similar way, we can measure with the arrangement shown in Fig. 55, the vertical component, *ov*, of the wind pressure, taking care that the spring balance is so adjusted that the lever oscillates around the horizontal. Fig. 56 illustrates how, by combining *oh* and *ov*, we obtain the resultant force *or*, which, in magnitude and direction, represents the result of the wind pressure on the surface *ab*.

Of course, surface *ab* must possess the same inclination towards the horizon in both cases, and the forces must relate to the same wind velocity.

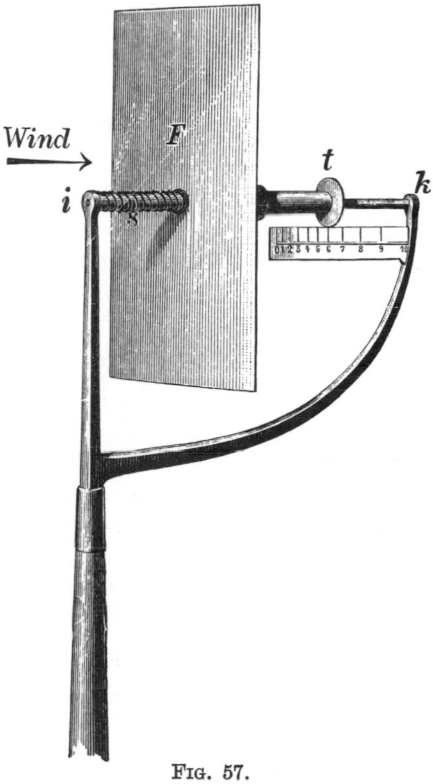

For the measurement

FIG. 57.

of this wind velocity, the apparatus shown in Fig. 57 may be employed. It consists of the plate F, constructed as a wooden frame covered with paper. This plate slides freely on the rod *ik*, and is connected with the end *i* by means of the spiral spring *s*.

When the plate F is subjected to the forces of the wind, it will slide along the rod and indicate the speed by means of the index *t*, which passes over a scale calibrated directly in velocities.

From the area of the plate F, it is easy to calculate the wind pressure which exists at various wind velocities, and since the elasticity of the spiral spring is known, it is possible to calibrate the scale with accuracy.

The indicator which we employed had an area F equal to $\frac{1}{10}$ of a square metre; it must be placed close to the apparatus, Figs. 54 and 55, in order to be able at any instant to determinate the wind velocity existing near the test surface.

It is best if three persons are available for this experiment, one reading the wind velocity, another reading the spring scale and a third noting down the figures called out by the two observers. The wind velocity varies almost every second, but sometimes it remains constant for several seconds. It is during these periods of uniformity that the one observer must call out the velocity and the second observer the respective wind pressure. After having carried out a large number of measurements first for the one and then for the other component, we obtain useful figures from the mean values and finally from the two components, and for various inclinations of the surface we arrive at the actual air pressure.

The first experiments which we carried out with this description of apparatus date from the year 1874. We used surfaces laterally pointed with an area of $\frac{1}{4}$ sq. m. and a camber. Our experimental ground was situated on the vast plain between Charlottenburg and Spandau, which has now become a racecourse, and which was suitable for our purpose.

To check this experiment we again measured the wind pressure in the autumn of 1888, using surfaces as shown in Fig. 47. In this case we installed our apparatus on the equally unobstructed plain between Teltow, Zehlendorf, and Lichterfelde, not far from the Military Academy.

The results of both experiments, although they refer to different constructions and different sizes, are in good accord. The relation of the wind pressure for the various inclinations of the surface against the horizon are plodded as usual on Plate V., Fig. 1. Taking the camber as $\frac{1}{12}$ of the width, Fig. 2 on Plate V. shows the deviations of the air pressure direction from the perpendicular to the surface.

Since we have drawn these curves on the same scale as

formerly, it is possible to compare the last diagrams with the former ones, besides which we have drawn a diagram on Plate IV. in dotted lines, and it is at once evident how greatly the result of this wind experiment differs from those obtained by rotating surfaces in calm air.

This difference is most pronounced for the small inclinations, especially at the inclination of zero. The horizontal curved surface is lifted by the wind and not pushed back, and this fact, which directly explains the sailing flight of birds, will have to be fully dealt with later on.

It is desirable to find an explanation of the vast difference in wind pressure between that condition in which the surface rotates with the given velocity and that in which this same surface is held at the same inclination in the wind with the same velocity.

The following experiments will furnish the necessary data for this explanation.

§ XXXIII.—The Increase of Lifting Effect due to Wind.

On endeavouring to determine the vertical components according to Fig. 55, and after placing the surface ab into the direction of

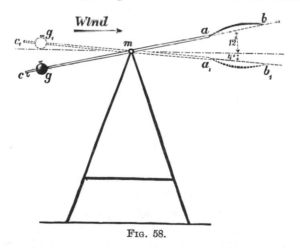

FIG. 58.

the lever cma (Fig. 58), and balancing it by means of g, we find that on leaving the arrangement to itself in a wind, the lever does not "play in" horizontally, but that the surface swings slightly up and down, and is so lifted that its mean position is about 12° above the horizontal. To pull down the surface until it assumes a horizontal position requires a relatively great force, about equal to one-half of the air resistance of the area when moved vertically against the wind. In position *cmab*, therefore, the surface is balanced by the wind. If we now reverse the surface so that the concave side is upward, the system assumes the position shown by the dotted line, $c_1ma_1b_1$; that is to say, the lever end, which carries the surface, is lowered by about 4° on the average below the horizon. From this we conclude that a surface without any curvature, *i.e.* a plane, should assume such a position that angle ama_1 is bisected. This experiment we have actually made on several occasions, and we found that the above conclusion was proved by the experiment, the lever with the plane surface assuming an inclination of about 3–4° above the horizon (Fig. 59). There was again the usual see-saw movement, but the

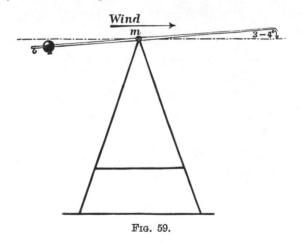

Fig. 59.

medium position could be easily determined. All this explains the strong lifting components observed in the wind ; the effect is as though the wind blew slantingly upward.

Apparatus Fig. 59 represents a kind of weather vane with horizontal axis, and, when placed close to buildings, shows considerable variations of wind in the vertical plane. At such places the ascending and descending wind directions change very suddenly, frequently producing oscillations of 90° and more on the lever. On extensive, bare plains, however, there is far greater constancy in this respect, though we always find slight variations above and below the mean position of about 3·5°. It is a remarkable fact that this phenomenon is almost unaffected, even if we erect the lever on rising or falling ground, provided only that the whole of the experimental ground is fairly horizontal. We were able to find the same position of the lever, even if the ground dropped 5° in the wind direction for more than 200 m.

Our numerous experiments convinced us that this property of wind effect is extremely constant, and is very little influenced by wind direction, strength, season or hour.

In all probability this is due to the increase of the wind velocity towards the upper strata. When the speed indicator registers in the open field a velocity of 4 m. at 1 m. from the ground, it often registers 7 m. at a height of 3 m. We need not pause for an explanation of this ascending wind direction; it is sufficient for us to know for the theory of birdflight and for aviation that wind exerts such an effect upon surfaces as though they were tilted 3°–4° upward.

In order to obtain still further corroboration of this very vital fact, we designed an apparatus, represented in Fig. 60, carrying five vanes, with horizontal axes, and arranged at levels of 2, 4, 6, 8, and 10 m. above ground.

All the five levers showed the tilt of 3°–4°, but their instantaneous positions varied singly or simultaneously in strength and direction. In order to produce a uniform effect, we joined the levers on both sides of their axes by means of fine wires (see Fig. 60), whereby they were forced to remain parallel and to give us the mean wind tilt up to 10 m. above ground, a tilt which likewise varied incessantly around the 3°–4° positive inclination. To eliminate all possible errors, we made the arrangement self-registering in the manner shown by Fig. 60; the bottom lever transferred its movements, by means of a light rod, to a tracing pencil on a paper chart, fixed to a drum, which was revolved with uniform velocity, and produced a wave-line. The zero-line was obtained by adjusting the levers horizontally with a spirit level and by once revolving the drum.

In this manner we obtained diagrams which clearly showed

the mean tilt of the wind. Fig. 3 on Plate V. is a reproduction of such a diagram (of one minute's duration), and we find that the tracer was generally above the zero-line, and oscillated between 10 and 5; the maximum variations which we observed on a large level plain, but which were of rare occurrence, lay between 16

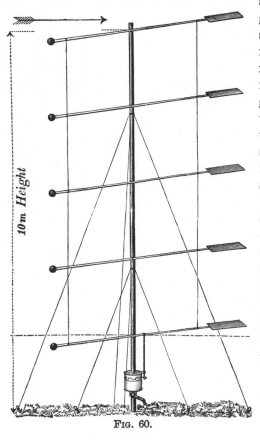

10m Height

and 9. All the diagrams thus obtained showed certain common characteristics; for a duration of one minute they almost all gave the same mean value of 3·3, and the tracing pencil descends several times during a minute, though for only a very short time, below the zero-line. For the same period, all the curves agreed practically in the number of maxima and minima (20 of each), so that the ascending and descending tendency persists for about three seconds; only in exceptional cases was there an approximate constancy in the tilt persisting for six to eight seconds. This

FIG. 60.

clearly shows what difficulties we encounter when experimenting on air resistances in the wind, and that it is only by dint of very numerous experiments that we can obtain useful mean values. We should also mention that the vanes generally tilted, whilst we, who were sitting at the base of the apparatus, felt very little wind, so that we must assume comparatively great differences in the velocity towards a higher altitude. If, on the other hand, the wind blew stronger near the ground, the vanes generally tilted downwards. This was *not* an *invariable* fact, however, and we are not justified in basing any deduction upon the observation.

The increase in the wind towards higher strata must be necessarily accompanied by a rolling movement, extending more or less through the whole air mass, since it is unlikely that air-layers of different velocities glide rectilinearly above each other without influencing each other by friction, although the increase of wind velocity may be very gradual. As a result we may presume the paths of the air particles to be cycloidical waves made somewhat irregular, owing to the irregularities of the ground, and which can only maintain their uniform character in longer periods.

The friction of the moving air at the surface of the ground, the differences of temperature and the equalizations of pressure which always compel the wind in the direction in which accumulations of the atmosphere are required, all these factors explain the constant variations in the features of the wind and its properties.

Finally, we support the view that the line described by the smoke-column from a tall, isolated factory chimney during windy weather, is an excellent guide to the air movement and its ascending direction. It may be objected that this ascent is due to the hot products of combustion ; but this latter cause can only act in the immediate vicinity of the chimney, and cannot extend over stretches measured in kilometres.

In order to investigate the real relation between all the above-mentioned phenomena and their supposed causes, and for the purpose of deducting actual laws, it is necessary to considerably extend the experiments, and especially to take into consideration simultaneously with the variations in wind tilt, the variations in lateral direction, in strength and its increase with the level. Exhaustive experiments on these lines would be most desirable and of the greatest importance not only to aviators but also to meteorologists.

§ XXXIV.—Air Pressure on the Bird's Wing in Calm Air, deduced from Measurements in Wind.

We may assume that in the experiments which gave us the diagram on Plate V., the wind possessed a mean ascending direction of at least 3°; in order, therefore, to compare the results of wind measurements with those obtained on the whirling machine, we have to add 3° to the inclinations adjusted for the former case. This gives us Fig. 1, Plate VI., in which, for comparison, the corresponding line of Plate IV. has been marked in dots.

We can now appreciate the difference between the two modes of experimenting. The discrepancies are due to the errors introduced by the whirling machine, and which we have mentioned before. Plate VI. represents the air pressure upon a surface similar in shape to the wing of a bird, and moved in a straight line in air. These lines, as well as those caused by wind, are drawn in their relative magnitudes at the top of Plate VII., and again we perceive how greatly the pressure is increased by curvature of the surface. But it is not alone the *magnitude* of this air pressure which is a measure of the effect: to an almost greater extent the *direction* of the air pressure influences the result.

For this purpose we employ Fig. 1, Plate VI., and imagine the horizontal curved surface *ab* moved downwards in the directions 0°–90°.

Fig. 2 on Plate VI., deducted from the wind experiments, shows the actual directions of the air pressures to surface *ab*, whilst the latter moves along a straight line in calm air.

§ XXXV.—The Energy required for Flight in Calm Air as deducted from the Wind Experiments.

We can calculate the economy in energy due to forward flight in still air, and obtain the values which are shown in Fig. 2, Plate VI., alongside the respective angles of the mean direction in which the wings are moved; these are compared with the energy A necessary when flight is stationary. The minimum of energy is required when the wings move very rapidly forward and slowly downward, *i.e.* for comparatively quick flight. Even taking into account the air resistance on the body of the bird, we find that the necessary energy is barely $\frac{1}{10}$ of that for stationary flight, owing to the very slow downward beat of the wings. The advantage accruing from beating motion will, however, be considerably reduced.

According to § XVIII., the minimum exertion for stationary human flight is 1 h.p., but by reason of the partial loss of the "beat advantage" this might even work out at 3 h.p. (Plate VI.). For flight with a mean value of 3° wing inclination, the mechanical effort for a human being would be 0·3 h.p. This amount of energy is within the possibilities of human effort especially after some training. Given a very favourable shape for the flying apparatus, with 15 to 20 sq. m. area, and not more than 22 lbs. weight, rapid horizontal flight in still air becomes feasible.

But, at any rate, with such an apparatus and without beating the wings, we can execute a prolonged downward glide, which would present plenty of interest and instruction.

§ XXXVI. — Surprising Phenomena observed when experimenting with Curved Surfaces in the Wind.

A study of the diagrams on Plates V. and VI. of course impresses upon our mind that great importance of the peculiar effect of wind on curved surfaces, yet this impression is not as strong as that made upon the experimenter who first plodded these diagrams.

The law of air pressure, as expressed in these diagrams, may be considered the key to many phenomena observed in connection with birdflight, and it is therefore of importance to single out the more unusual facts which have been found out by the experiments to which we owe these diagrams.

Whoever undertakes such experiments will receive many impressions which cannot be recorded by mere figures and graphic diagrams only; the effects of forces which, in addition to seeing and hearing one also actually feels, leave a very much stronger impression as regards their importance for the object aimed at.

For this reason, it is extremely instructive to experiment with properly formed large wings in the wind. All those, however, who have no opportunity for such experiments may be interested in the following notes :—

When first we entered the wind with such lightly constructed wings, our theoretical notion of the significance of curved wings immediately became a certainty. Already when carrying such large wings to the experimenting ground interesting observations can be made; though it is a matter for satisfaction to have a strong wind blowing, because the accuracy of the observations is greater when the numerical values are greater, yet the transport of the experimental surfaces across an open field, with a strong wind blowing, causes difficulties.

The surfaces are, for instance, composed of light willow canes, covered on each side with paper, and great care in handling is required anyhow; but with the wind pressing upon them in an erratic manner, at one instant in one direction and then in another, one does not know how to carry these surfaces. The very first transport teaches us certain tricks; we find that such a curved surface, which, when carried with the concave side uppermost, is as heavy as though it had been filled with sand, when turned the other way round—namely, with the concave side downwards—is lifted by the wind and nearly carried.

If we place the hand lightly upon the surface so as to prevent it from ascending, and if we take care that its horizontal position is maintained, we find that it practically floats on the wind, and a surface with an area of 0·5 sq. m. makes it possible to support part of the weight of one's arm when the wind is strong.

Now, with the diagrams before us, it is an easy matter to calculate the lifting effect upon such a surface with the wind blowing with a velocity of 10 metres. If we only assume that half the pressure is employed for lifting, then, under the above-mentioned conditions, we obtain an air pressure of—

$$L = \tfrac{1}{2} \times 0\cdot13 \times 0\cdot5 \times 100 = 3\cdot25 \text{ kg.}$$

Suppose the weight of the surface is 1·25 kg., then we have to actually press down upon it with a force of 2 kg. to prevent it

from being lifted by the wind. One feels the surface floating on
the wind, but we need not fear that the wind would carry it away
in its direction, because the air pressure is directed vertically
upward, and there is no drifting tendency if the surface is well
shaped and the camber about $\frac{1}{12}$ of the width. This is always a
matter of great surprise for those who are not accustomed to these
experiments. One has the impression that if the surface were
only correspondingly larger—say 20 sq. m. instead of 0·5 sq. m.—
one could, without difficulty, sail away by its aid. Of course,
the equilibrium has to be studied, and we are reminded that
considerable practice is necessary in order to direct such large
surfaces with certainty in the wind.

When the frame illustrated in Fig. 55 has been erected, and
the test surface has been so fixed that its edges lie in the direction
of the lever, *i.e.* that the surface is horizontal when the lever is
horizontal, even a gentle wind will give to the surface a tendency
to rise, because the weight of the surface has been compensated
by the counterweight.

On releasing the surface, the end of the lever to which the
surface is fixed rises still higher, as already described in
§ XXXIII. In the course of measurements of force we note
the large divergences from the results obtained when employing flat surfaces. We are struck by the lifting effect of the
wind on such curved surfaces, even when the leading edge
of the surface is at a lower level than the trailing edge. The
lifting effect, as we have seen from the diagram on Plate VI.,
only ceases when the chord of the surface has a downward
inclination of 12° against the wind direction; this is a condition
under which one would expect that the wind would strongly
depress the surface.

After having determined the vertical components of the wind
pressure, we place the lever in a vertical position in order to note
the horizontal pressures (Fig. 54). Beginning with a horizontal
adjustment of the surface a new surprise awaits us. Contrary
to all expectation, the lever with the large test surface on top
remains vertical, or oscillates only slightly around this vertical
position, even during the heaviest gale. The projection of the
surface in the direction of the wind, including the thickness of
the surface, amounts to one-tenth of its whole base, and yet the

wind does not push the surface backward! On displacing the lever from its vertical position, both towards the wind and away from the wind, the test surface always returns to its highest position, *i.e.* the lever "plays in" vertically. This proves that the surface is not only *able* to maintain its highest position, but that it *must* maintain this position, and that it is therefore in stable equilibrium.

We can enhance this impression when we fix some heavy

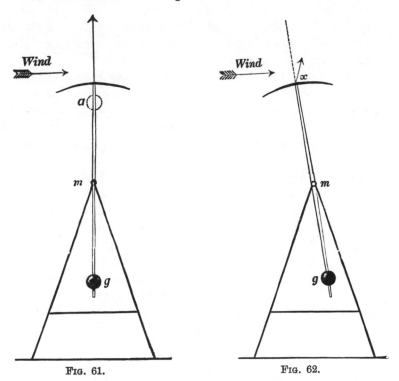

FIG. 61.   FIG. 62.

object, for example, a stone (ours weighed 2 kgs.), to the lever below the test surface, so as to render the upper half of the lever heavier than the lower half, but even under these conditions the surface retains its stable position, provided we do not exceed a certain limit with regard to the weight of the stone for a given force of wind.

With the diagram of Plate V. before us it is not difficult to explain this phenomenon. We perceive that for an inclination of 0° against the horizon the wind pressure is normal to the surface, that is to say, is directed vertically upward, but that for negative angles, *i.e.* if the surface is inclined downward against the wind, the wind pressure acts, in a pushing sense upon the surface. The position, Fig. 62, therefore results in a wind pressure which endeavours to pull the surface back into its middle position. For positions such as shown in Fig. 63, and for angles up to 30°, the wind pressure is represented by y, and lies windward, relative to the perpendicular to the surface. This force likewise tends to bring the surface into the middle position, in which the wind pressure on a horizontal surface acts vertically upward. This result, which of course was unknown before, demonstrates most clearly the suitability of slightly curved wings for sailing flight, that is to say, for a flight without wing-movement, and without any appreciable dynamical effort on the part of the flying bird. The surface of which we have just spoken would ascend if it were not fixed to the lever and if one could secure its horizontal position, a demand which would be best satisfied by making the surface the wing of a living creature.

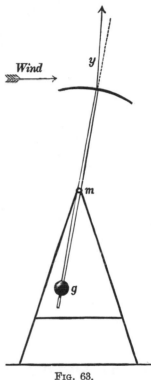

Fig. 63.

Birds which are capable of sailing flight are able to remain stationary in the air, resting upon the wind, as we can often observe when the falcon looks for his prey and searches the ground; but they can also sail against the wind, not only in circular paths, but also in straight lines. We have often noticed, when investigating the causes which make such sailing flights possible, that the birds floated towards the wind at a considerable altitude. Our own experiments place the fact beyond doubt that there are surfaces which are lifted vertically by the wind, and are not pushed back, but the birds show us that there must exist some peculiar surface, which, at least in the higher strata, is pulled towards the wind, *i.e.* which, when stationary with respect to the ground, must show a wind pressure not only vertically directed upward, but somewhat towards the wind; it is this property which enables the bird to overcome the resistance of its body. This peculiarity can at first only be explained by assuming the wind to have an ascending direction; but a real investigation of the fact can only be commenced when we are able to feel the wind pressure acting upon our own experimental wings whilst suspended in mid-air.

What we have stated in this section with regard to wing surfaces may be applied partially to all other curved surfaces which are exposed to the wind. We come across many observations in daily life which mark the peculiar properties of wind on curved surfaces.

The linen which is placed on a rope in order to dry, as well as any flag which flies from a horizontal pole, demonstrate the strong lift which curved surfaces experience in wind, and which pushes them even above the horizontal position (see Fig. 64). We also

FIG. 64.

find frequent applications of the aerodynamical advantages of curves surfaces in many other ways. The sails of ships, as well as the sails of Dutch windmills, owe a great part of their efficiency to the curvature of their surfaces, a curvature which they either assume by themselves or which has been given to them.

Having seen what enormous differences exist when a surface, upon which the wind impinges at a very acute angle, assumes even a slight curvature, we can understand that on calculating the sailing capacity of ships on the basis of flat sails, we only obtain a very rough approximation of actual results, which latter far surpass our calculations.

The constant fluttering, in a strong wind, of flags which are mounted on vertical poles, can also be explained by the peculiarities of curved surfaces.

A stiff weather-vane, made of sheet metal, places itself in the wind direction, but not so a flag made of soft material. Fig. 65 shows the plan of a weather-vane.

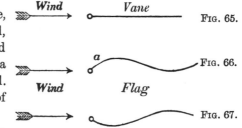

Fig. 65.

Fig. 66.

Fig. 67.

The soft flag, however, executes sinuous movements, which may be explained as follows :—

Such flags are in unstable equilibrium, because the slightest curvature to one side increases the wind pressure upon this side, and in consequence the curvature becomes more pronounced (Fig. 66). If the wind pressure at *a* becomes sufficiently great, then this curvature is pushed through to the other side, and the shape of the flag changes to that shown in Fig. 67, and so the play continues.

We may also in this place draw attention to the fact that every boomerang, which is usually of the cross-section shown in Fig. 68, can be very much improved if we hollow out one surface as shown in Fig. 69.

We also find that Nature utilizes the advantage of curved wings even in the vegetable kingdom, by providing the seeds of certain plants with slightly curved wings, so as to enable them to sail along in the wind.

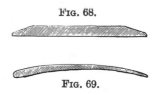

Fig. 68.

Fig. 69.

It may be of interest to experiment with slightly curved surfaces under water. Even on a very small scale we can obtain some results ; as, for instance, when we move a spoon in a cup full of liquid we can already notice the tendency for the spoon to move in the direction of this curvature. We may assume that the speculations which we have made in § XXV. in connection with Fig. 39, apply to a certain degree for movements under water, and the question arises whether there is not a gap in the theory of the marine propeller, because this camber of the cross-section has not been given sufficient attention to.

§ XXXVII.—The Possibility of Sailing Flight.

The experiments which we described in the foregoing section demonstrate that certain properties of curved surfaces with regard to wind pressure make actual sailing in the air a possibility. The sailing bird, a kite liberated from its string, are things of reality and not of the imagination.

Probably not every one who is interested in the mechanism of birdflight has had the opportunity of so closely observing large sailing birds that the conviction of the absence of effort in such flight could take root, but there are many observers who are fully aware that the ease with which birds can sail is a most marvellous yet indisputable fact.

As already mentioned, foremost amongst the birds who are masters of this kind of flight are the birds of prey, marsh birds, and sea fowl. It is, however, not proved that other species of birds are incapable of sailing flight, though their mode of living does not induce them to exercise this ability. I was at one time much surprised to notice a flock of crows sailing perfectly at a considerable altitude and for an extended period, having assumed that real sailing flight of crows was unknown.

The exact method of sailing differs somewhat among the various species. Birds of prey generally circle, but these circles are not closed, but form in combination with the movement of the wind, cycloidical curves, and it appears as though this is the easiest method of sailing, since all birds who sail at all employ this method.

It is not improbable that, thanks to the somewhat inclined position of these sailing paths, the difference in the velocity of the wind at various altitudes may assist in supporting the bird, but this factor is too small to explain by itself sailing flight. We know that the lifting effect of wind on suitably curved wings accounts for the ascent of birds without wing-beats.

That the circling motion is of secondary importance is evidenced by the fact that birds "sail" without that motion. How can we explain the immobility in a wind of the falcon, an immobility persisted in for minutes? That this feat is particularly difficult is obvious, since there are few land birds which are capable of it. The object of the falcon is, of course, to be as unobtrusive as possible, while scanning from above the ground for prey, and we frequently noticed how he suddenly swooped down from such a position.

Birds inhabiting the moors and marshes appear to employ "circling" chiefly to attain greater altitudes, in which they find the wind of such strength as to enable them to properly "sail": "circling," as we have seen, being easier to accomplish, and requiring therefore less wind. When arrived at a sufficiently high level, the bird often sails in a direct line towards its goal. Storks likewise execute these manœuvres. Birds living near the coast and on the sea are particularly masters of these tricks; their wing form seems to be pre-eminently fitted for sailing flight, and they practise every method of sailing, including motionless "hovering" in the wind.

All these movements call for no special motive power, but only for properly shaped wings and the skill or "feeling" to adapt the wing position to the wind.

It is probable that our experimental surfaces, even though they had the properties necessary for "sailing," were not provided with those details which perfect "sailing" requires.

We are therefore not justified in considering the series of investigations as complete, though they have shown us that a continuance in the same direction will amply repay the labour, and will finally enable us to fully understand the most ideal of all forms of locomotion, namely, free sailing in air, not only in its application to birdflight, but to human flight.

Recapitulating, we must, in the first instance, consider the proper wing curvature as the means of making sailing flight possible: only those wings, the cross-section of which shows a suitable camber, produce such a favourable direction of the air pressure as to avoid any appreciable restraining component. But another factor is also essential; the properties of the surface alone are not sufficient to allow of continued sailing; there must be a wind of at least medium velocity which, by its ascending direction, so alters the direction of the pressure, that the bird becomes comparable to a free kite, moving towards the wind.

The following few experiments also shed some light on these points.

We have repeatedly made some kites which resemble birds, not only in the outline, but also in that their wing sections were curved like those of birds' wings. Such kites behave differently from the ordinary paper kite, which, as is well known, shows peculiar characteristics according to construction.

To start with, a kite with cross-stay, as in Fig. 70, does not ascend so easily as one without. A side view will make the reason for this clear. Fig. 71, relating to the kite Fig. 70, shows two separate curvatures, but Fig. 72, which is the side view of a

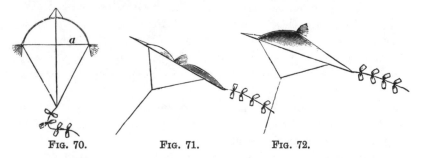

FIG. 70.   FIG. 71.   FIG. 72.

kite without cross-rib, shows there is only one larger curvature to either side of the axis, a curvature which endows the kite with a more favourable shape, since it is a closer approximation to the uniformly curved birds' wings.

Such a kite, even if flown in the same wind and with the same length of cord, ascends higher than that illustrated in Fig. 71, the reason being that kite Fig. 72 assumes a more horizontal position than kite Fig. 71, the ratio of lift to drift being greater in the former.

The excellent lifting power of the so-called "Japanese kite" is likewise due to the curvature of their wings.

If we desire a still higher ratio of lift to drift, we must shape the kite with the pointed outline of a bird. Fig. 73 shows how we formed our kites, *a, b, c,* and *d,* being willow canes fastened together and covered with shirting, with a cord binding at *e, f,* and g; such a kite assumed a nearly horizontal position with filled-out wings, and the holding cord is nearly vertical (Fig. 74).

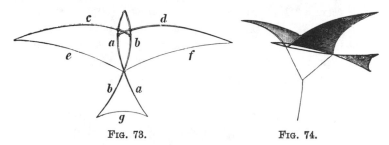

FIG. 73.   FIG. 74.

Still better results are attainable when making the wings of stiff material, so as not to have to depend upon the wind for their curvature; a number of curved, light ribs running crossways to the wings, ensure the proper curvature of the covering.

We fixed two cords, a and b, to a kite built on these lines (Fig. 75) in such a manner that we were able to vary the inclination of the kite at will. On bringing it into a horizontal position by pulling on cord a, the kite advanced towards the wind without descending, though we were unable to keep up this condition for

FIG. 75.

any length of time, because the cords sagged when the kite moved forward, and the slightest change in the wind upset the equilibrium. Only on one occasion, when there was a prolonged uniform wind, could we observe a continued free sailing against the wind.

The conditions were as follows :—

After several attempts to attain this free flotation, we released the cords and the kite flew against the wind (which showed a velocity of about 6 m.) without descending, travelling faster than we could when running as fast as possible against the wind. Unfortunately, after a run of about 50 m., one of the trailing cords became entangled in some undergrowth, disturbing the balance of the kite and bringing it down.

We returned home, after this experiment (September, 1874), with the conviction that sailing flight was not the exclusive prerogative of birds, but that the possibility of man flying in this manner was established, since no powerful movement of wings, but only a skilful direction of the wings, was required for the purpose.

§ XXXVIII.—The Bird as our Model.

From all the foregoing results it appears obvious that in order to discover the principles which facilitate flight, and to eventually enable man to fly, we must take the bird for our model.

We have seen that there are so many remarkable advantageous mechanical features in actual birdflight, that we would have to abandon all hope of flying if we would forego their employment.

It may therefore be permissible to once more investigate the phenomena characteristic of birdflight. Of course, in choosing birds as our model we shall not select those species the wings of which are almost rudimentary, such as is the case with some running birds. Small birds, likewise, such as the swallow, do not lend themselves for our purpose, though we may admire their skill and perfect mastership of flight; they are too small, and their incessant hunting for insects introduces too many erratic movements.

A specially suitable species of birds to act as our model is the sea-gull.

The best place for studying these birds is at the sea-shore, because not being hunted, they are very friendly with man, and disport themselves at close quarters. We are therefore able to clearly distinguish every movement of their wings, and knowing the peculiar properties of air pressure in connection with birds' wings, we may gradually solve some of the problems connected with their beautiful method of flight. What applies to the gull, applies more or less to all other birds and flying creatures.

How does the gull fly? As a rule the air near the sea is disturbed, and this enables the gull to sail along, only assisting from time to time with a few wing-beats, but rarely circling, now turning to the right and now to the left, ascending, descending, the head inclined, and constantly scanning the sea for food.

At the very first glance we notice that the slender, slightly curved wings execute a peculiar motion, in so far as only the wing-tips move appreciably up and down, whilst the broader arm-portions near the body take little part in this movement, a condition of things which is illustrated in Fig. 76.

Does not this peculiarity show us another means of facilitating flight, and of reducing the necessary expenditure of energy? May we not assume that the comparatively motionless parts of the wings enable the gull to sail along, whilst the tips, consisting of easily rotating feathers, serve to compensate for the loss of forward velocity? It is unmistakable that the wide portion of the wing

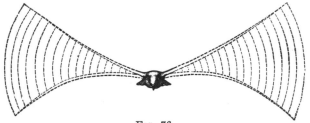

Fig. 76.

close to the body, which does little work and has little movement, is intended for sustaining, whilst the narrower tips, with their much greater amplitude of movement, have to furnish the tractive power necessary to compensate for the resistance of the bird's body and for any possible restraining component.

This being conceded, we are forced to consider the flying apparatus of the bird as a most ingenious and perfect mechanism, which has its fulcrum in the shoulder joint, which moves up and down, and by virtue of its articulation permits of increased lift or fall as well as of rotation of the light tips.

The arm portion of the wing is heavy, containing bones, muscles, and tendons, and therefore opposes considerable inertia to any rapid movement. But it is well fitted for supporting, because being close to the body, the air pressure upon it acts on a short lever arm, and the bending strain is therefore less severe on the wing. The tip is very light, consisting of feathers only, and can be lifted and depressed in rapid succession. If the air pressure produced by it increased in proportion to the greater amplitude of movement, it would require a large amount of work, and would also unduly strain the wings; we therefore conclude that the real function of the wing-tips is not so much the generation of a great lifting effect, but rather the production of a smaller, but tractive effect directed forward.

In fact, actual observation leaves no doubt on this point. It is only necessary to watch the gull during sunshine, and from the light effects we can distinctly perceive the changing inclination of the wing-tips, as shown in Figs. 77 and 78, which refer

Up-stroke.

FIG. 77.

to the upstroke and downstroke of the wings respectively. The gull, flying away from us, presents at the upstroke, Fig. 77, the upper side of its wings strongly illuminated by the sun, whilst during the downstroke (Fig. 78) we have the shaded camber presented to us from the back. The tip evidently ascends with

Down-stroke.

FIG. 78. (GULL IN FLIGHT.)

the leading edge raised, and descends with the leading edge depressed, both phases resulting in a tractive effect.

Also, when flying past us, the gull will enable a trained observer to judge of the wing-tips.

Fig. 79 illustrates the gull just before beating its wings downward; towards the tip the wing has the cross-section *acb* which is inclined forward, and the absolute path of which is represented by line *cd*, whilst *ce* is the resulting air pressure. The simultaneous lifting and tractive effect of the latter is clearly noticeable.

It is not so certain whether all parts of the wing play a similar part during the upstroke; if it were so, then it would also imply a downward pressing effect. Perhaps it is so more especially when the bird desires to attain very great speed.

The upstroke may also take place under such an inclination

that there is no pressure at all, either from above or from below, and finally it is possible that a peculiar kind of upstroke may produce a lifting effect, in which particular case we have the remarkable condi-

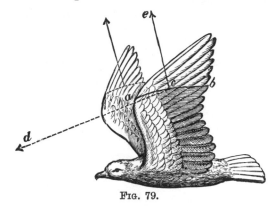

Fig. 79.

tion for which all parts of the wing act in a lifting sense during the whole period of flight—a condition which, as we have seen in a previous section, influences the possible saving of work in the most effective manner.

Of course, the upstroke will produce less lift than the down-stroke, yet if the former results in only so much pressure from below that it lifts the wing and compensates for its mass inertia, it helps the bird, because practically no force is then necessary to lift the wings.

It is also possible that the air pressure (during forward flight) upon the lifted and warped wing is so distributed as to produce a lift on the arm portion, whilst the effect on the wing-tips is of a tractive nature, as indicated in Fig. 80. In this case the detri-

Fig. 80.

mental downward components acting upon the tips are compensated and overcome by the upward components on the broader part of the same wing.

H

We can therefore imagine that during this kind of flight, even during the upstroke of the wings, there still exists a partial lifting effect, that no diminution of the flight velocity takes place, and that there remains, possibly, even a small forward propelling pressure.

A simple calculation will prove that the above considerations are correct. Compare the rise and fall of the centre of gravity of a bird which was supposed to be only lifted during the downstroke of the wings, with the actual rise and fall as determined by observation.

A large gull rises and falls, even during a calm, barely 3 cm., although with $2\frac{1}{2}$ wing beats per second this figure would be 10 cm., if it were based upon all the lifting effect being due to down-strokes only.

The sinusoidal curve, Fig. 81, represents the absolute path of the

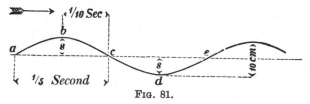

FIG. 81.

centre of gravity for a seagull executing the upstroke of the wing without appreciable resistance, but also without lifting effect.

Assuming an equal period for the up and downstroke, each would occupy $\frac{1}{5}$ second. The gull commences to lift its wings at a; the initial upward speed diminishes under the influence of its weight, and is converted into a downward velocity, so that the path of the centre of gravity describes the parabola abc, during the period of wing lift, i.e. during $\frac{1}{10} + \frac{1}{10}$ second. In accordance with the law of gravity the distance s for the time t equals, $s = \frac{1}{2}gt^2$, g standing for 9.81, and (for the gull) $t = \frac{1}{10}$ sec.

$$s = \frac{1}{2} \, 9.81 \times \tfrac{1}{100} = 0.05 \text{ m.} = 5 \text{ cm.}$$

From c the play of the wings is reversed, the latter beating downward and producing an air pressure equal to twice the weight of the bird, so that the remaining lifting force equals the weight of the gull. The centre of gravity now describes the negative curve *cde*, for which *s* also equals 5 cm., thus giving a total of 10 cm. for rise and fall, as above stated.

The result of the calculation will be somewhat different when assuming a less time for the upstroke than for the downstroke; but even if we apply only $\frac{2}{5}$ of the whole period to the former phase, the centre of gravity still moves more than 6 cm., and we are forced to assume the existence of a lifting component during the upstroke of the wings in order to reconcile calculation and observation.

This property of wings constitutes a further facilitating factor in flight, and is an advantage accruing from the up and down movement of the wings in which the amplitude increases from the root to the tip.

Every part of the wing therefore moves in a different, absolute path. The parts close to the body barely rise or fall, but possess essentially only a horizontal velocity, and their function corresponds to that of the whole wing in "sailing" flight; their position should therefore be such as to produce a maximum of lifting pressure without undue restraining component. The unavoidable retardation of forward flight, chiefly due to the body itself, is compensated by the oblique forward pressure which results from the fact that the wing tips automatically assume a forward inclined position during the down-beat and the latter portion of their absolute path, a pressure which suffices for the maintenance of the desired forward speed.

During the upstroke of the wing, the wing portions close to the body continue to act as supporting planes, but the parts near the tip, which execute a greater movement, and the absolute path of which is directed obliquely upward, will be so turned that they may attain the top position as quickly as possible, and without experiencing much resistance. We can therefore imagine that the various parts of the wing describe lines of a different amplitude (as shown in Fig. 82), and the several wing sections assume positions, and produce air pressures, similar to those shown in this illustration. It is assumed that all parts of the wing produce a lift during the upstroke.

The resultant force of these air pressures must be large enough and so directed that they balance the weight of the bird, as well as the air resistance opposed to the body of the bird.

For this purpose it is necessary that the bird's wing rotates during the upstroke and downstroke, very little near the root, and considerably near the tip. This rotation will take place when the

FIG. 82.

direction of the stroke is reversed, and since this reverse always takes a certain amount of time, we may assume that there is a small loss; it will decrease as the wings decrease in width. As an example, we would mention the albatross, the wings of which have a width of only about $\frac{1}{10}$ of their length, and which are shown on p. xxii, in $\frac{1}{30}$ scale. This may be the reason why Nature has resolved the tips of the wings into pinions in those birds which have very wide wings; the dense part of the wing is only called upon to execute very small rotations, whilst the large rotation is executed by each pinion singly.

These single pinions form, as it were, narrow curved wings, which, in order to rotate freely, must not overlap. Every observer of the flight of storks will have noticed this play of the feathers, since during the two phases of the wing movement, one is able to periodically see through the wings.

Fig. 83, which illustrates such a pinion from a condor, shows how carefully Nature designed them. Near the root, the pinion is

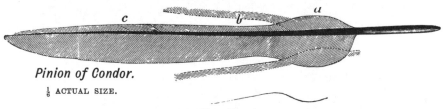

Pinion of Condor.
$\frac{1}{6}$ ACTUAL SIZE.

FIG. 83.

75 mm. wide, and at the point a it has the cross-section shown in Fig. 84, a section which is peculiarly capable of reaching below the adjacent feather, and so to form a closed surface.

The part of the pinion towards the end of the quill is narrower on both sides, namely, 48 mm. wide at b, and 55 mm.

at *c*. Fig. 85 gives the section through this narrower part, which almost represents a separate wing. The figure is drawn to actual

FIG. 84.　　　　　　　　　　　FIG. 85.

size, and well illustrates the parabolic curvature assumed when the bird is circling in the air. Such pinions are so rigid that, although they may bend in the direction of their length, their cross-section changes but very little.

If we treat such a feather in accordance with § XXVII., Fig. 45, we find that it shows a torsion which commences at the quill and increases towards the tip; this torsion is brought about by the fact that the posterior beard is about six times as wide as the anterior. This feature is in perfect accord with the function of the feather, *i.e.* to produce air pressures which have a forward tractive effect.

Thus we see that every single pinion is really intended to be a small separate wing, which is able to execute the necessary movements, especially rotations.

This is very clearly to be seen in Figs. 86 and 87, which

Up-stroke.

FIG. 86.

represent the mechanism of the wing of a condor during the upstroke and downstroke.

Another point which is indicative of the separate effect of

Down-stroke.

Section through pinion.
FIG. 87.

these single pinions is their greater width towards the end (see point *c*, Fig. 83), a feature which evidently enables the surface to be more perfectly utilized.

This rotation of the pinions is not entirely due to the tendons

and muscles of the bird, nor does the difference in the degree of
tension of the follicles in which the quill is inserted, account for
the whole of this effect ; possibly the rotation is assisted by some
effect in connection with the difference existing between the width
of the beard on each side of the quill.

Nature never introduces any feature without a purpose : the
construction of these feathers obviously indicates their use, and
shows them to be the resolution of a large, wide, and close wing
into several narrow and easily rotating wings, which do not
overlap, so that the posterior, wider beards are able to rotate
into their proper position on the down-beat, if not by muscular
effort on the part of the bird, then at least automatically by the
wind pressure.

This is one of the chief characteristics, applying to the pinion
mechanism of all the larger birds of prey and marsh birds, which
allows of no other interpretation.

We cannot leave this subject without once more reverting to
that bird which seems to have been created for the purpose of
serving as a model for human flight, one of the largest species of
birds inhabiting our continent, a past master of every type
of flight, and one whom we have unique opportunities of observing
in his natural state, and in the full freedom of his movements.
We refer to the stork, which, being born upon our housetops,
spending there his early youth, and receiving his flying lessons
from his parents in the air above us, returns from his second home
in the far interior of Africa to visit our plains.

What is it which causes the stork to seek the company of man ?
Surely he is not in need of our protection, since he need not fear
any enemy in the animal kingdom. ; marten and cats, which might
menace his offspring, are more plentiful upon the roofs than in the
woods, though a thrust from his bill would soon despatch them.
The black stork, which, although easily tamed in captivity, is
not so fond of the human species, would leave him sufficient trees
whereon to build his nest firmly and safely, so that we cannot
imagine it to be the scarcity of likely refuges which causes the
bird to prefer the human habitations. Is he likely to be attracted
by the human voice or song, or does he appreciate other human
activities ? How is it possible to solve these questions without
gaining an understanding of the peculiar chattering of the bird ?

At any rate, this friendship and close association of man and stork dates back to remote, prehistoric times ; and we can only rejoice that—whatever the cause—one of the largest and most skilled flyers approaches man at a time when genial weather conditions invite us to spend our time in the open, and enable us to study his perfect flying movements.

The quiet village, rather than the big town, attracts the stork ; there he seems to be at ease, and to be most friendly to man. He seeks his food in closest proximity to the farm labourer. Not being able to walk in the high growth of the cornfields or to ascend from them, he follows in the wake of the harvester, and many a field mouse falls victim to him. This useful occupation is, in turn, appreciated by the farmer, who takes every possible care of the bird.

Thus it is not to be wondered at if the farmers, above whose homesteads these birds with a span of two metres hold great flight meetings every year, evince great interest in the art of flight, though they do not wish it to be known, fearing ridicule. Nevertheless, from no other trade or profession have so many inquiries for light engines—for a secret purpose—reached the author, as from farmers.

If there is much interest attached to the observation of the free living stork, the association with properly domesticated storks is full of interest and instruction. A young stork from the nest can be easily brought up on meat and fish, and soon gets attached to his keeper, becoming friendly to a high degree.

Many observations can be carried out whilst the young bird practises flight. Their home has been transferred from the roofs of distant villages to our garden, where they make themselves most useful by destroying field pests. It is but seldom that more than *one* young stork may be obtained from one nest, which as a rule contains four young birds, because the owners of the houses are greatly attached to the birds, and resent any molestation of the stork family. To obtain a number of storks, several nests, and generally several villages, have to be put under contribution. Especially when breeding from the domesticated birds, such pairing of storks from strange families is absolutely necessary, since the stork is averse to intermarriage, and birds from the same parents never pair.

When the actual flying practice begins, the first attention is devoted to the determination of the wind direction ; all the exercises are practised against the wind, but since the latter is not so constant on the lawn as on the roofs, progress is somewhat slower. Frequently, a sudden squall produces eddies in the air, and it is most amusing to watch the birds dancing about with lifted wings in order to catch the wind which changes from one side to another, all round. Any successful short flight is announced by joyful manifestations. When the wind blows uniformly from an open direction over the clearing, the young stork meets it, hopping and running, then turning round, he gravely walks back to the starting point and again tries to rise against the wind.

Such exercises are continued daily : At first only one single wing-beat succeeds, and before the wings can be raised for the second beat, the long, cautiously placed legs are again touching ground. But as soon as this stage is passed, *i.e.* when a second wing-beat is possible without the legs touching the ground, progress becomes very rapid, because the increased forward velocity facilitates flight, and three, four, or more double beats follow each other in one attempt, maybe awkward and unskilled, but never attended by accident, because of the caution exercised by the bird.

The same stork which we consider only a tyro under these circumstances, immediately attains security and endurance in flight when able to rise beyond the treetops where the fresh wind may be felt, and this fact very clearly demonstrates the importance of wind to birds, even young birds endeavouring to save themselves the effort of wing-beats, and resorting to " sailing " flight.

This unexpectedly rapid progress in flight of young storks on one occasion caused the loss to me of my three best flyers. Not believing such rapid development possible, and having to leave home for three days, I omitted to leave instructions regarding the locking up of the storks, although it was near the time of their departure south. On my return, I learned that during these three days, which were rather windy, the birds which before gave the impression of being much fatigued by their short, low flights, became flyers of endurance, and joined a swarm of passing storks on July 31.

On reproaching my people why they had not locked the birds

up, on seeing their high flights, they informed me that they flew
so beautifully, being able to rise higher and higher, and that their
soft black eyes pleaded so eloquently for the free enjoyment of
this ability, that they simply had not the heart to lock the birds up.

In a later section we shall calculate for the stork, our constant
model, how naturally the lifting effects develop, as soon as those
conditions are fulfilled which promote flight, *i.e.* when the wing
curvature, as actually measured, and the proper air pressures for
such curvatures are introduced into the calculation.

The knowledge of the phenomena of air resistance on wing-
shaped surfaces allows us, at least partly, to show the relation
between cause and effect in birdflight; we have learnt to construct
from the shape and movements of the wings, those forces which
actually enable the bird to be sustained in the air and to maintain
a velocity; we have seen in how far the long pointed or resolved
outline of the wings are of assistance, how the oscillating up and
down movement of the wings, accompanied by rotatory movements, concentrates the greatest lifting effect on the broad, upper
portion of the wing, etc., etc. Nature displays in these movements
a harmony of forces which must fill us with admiration, and shows
that it is useless to endeavour to reach by other means that which
nature attains so perfectly and simply by its own methods.

§ XXXIX.—The Balloon as an Obstacle.

Whilst the solution of the flight problem is, properly speaking,
the domain of the scientifically educated and practical, experienced
engineer, the whole question is one which engages the attention of
almost every other profession. Every one recognizes the extraordinary consequences which will attend the solution of the flight
problem; every one is able to see daily from the observations of
flying creatures that practical flight is possible. On the other
hand, no investigator has so far been found who can prove
conclusively that there is no hope for the imitation of flight
by man.

It is a remarkable fact that the very profession which is more
directly interested in the working out of the problem, takes a far
more indifferent attitude towards it than those to whom the

comprehension of the mechanism of birdflight presents some difficulty.

Activity in technical circles in this instance is very slight, and in no way consonant with the importance of the matter. Whilst in all technical departments we find pronounced system and order, the greatest want of order prevails in the department of technical flight; exchange of opinion is rare, and almost every specialist champions his own theory of flight.

The cause of this, as well as of the quite neglected condition of flight investigation, must be looked for in the discovery of the balloon. It may sound curious, but it is not superfluous to ask : What would have been the influence on the problem of mechanical flight if the balloon had not been discovered?

Apart from the fact that, in view of the progress of science, it is unthinkable that some investigator should not have utilized the buoyancy of light gases in the balloon, we may consider what would be the position of aerodynamical flight to-day if the aerostatic discovery had not been made.

Formerly, the only model for flight was the bird, but with the advent of the first balloon the whole question was placed on a different footing. It must have been intoxicating, when a century ago the first man actually rose from the earth into the air; and it is not a matter for surprise that then every one believed that the main difficulty was overcome, and that it required but a few improvements in order to steer the aerostat, which so safely effected the lifting into the air, in any desired direction, and so to utilize it for voluntary locomotion.

No wonder then that all the aim was directed towards making the balloon dirigible, and that especially in technical circles much attention was devoted to it. The actual tangible and alluring result was made the most of, and no one entertained the idea to again abandon the lifting power of the balloon, which was considered such a wonderful acquisition. What satisfaction it was, after striving for 10,000 years, that the ocean of the air had opened its unlimited space to us! It could not be difficult to utilize this new element for free locomotion, and it seemed as though it required very little, a mere detail, in order to completely solve the great problem of aerial navigation.

This detail has, in the meantime, shown itself to be an almost insurmountable difficulty, and we are arriving more and more at the conclusion that the balloon will remain what it is, namely, a means of rising in the air, but no means for practical and free navigation of the air.

Now that this conviction gains more ground, we return to the old standpoint, which the problem of aviation showed before the invention of the balloon, and the question naturally forces itself upon us how much further advanced we should have been with the problem of aviation if attention had not been diverted from it for 100 years, and if the abundant sacrifices of ingenuity and of money which were devoted to the attainment of the dirigible balloon had been applied to aviation.

The reply to such questions cannot be expressed in figures, but we cannot hide the fact that without the balloon we should have to record a greater amount of energy and interest as regards real aviation, and that the ruling scepticism which keeps those best fitted for its study away from aviation must be ascribed to the disappointment which the balloon caused us; but for this, much would be cleared up by now in this particular realm of science which so far is dark.

We are, therefore, justified in saying that the balloon has been of no assistance to real aviation; nay, it may even be considered as a direct brake upon the progress of this technique, because it split up the energy and directed the investigation which should have been devoted to dynamical flight into wrong channels.

This mistake has been brought about because there was a tendency to look for a gradual transition from the balloon to a flying machine capable of rapid free movements in air, whilst the balloon always remained the starting point, and through its unwieldy bulk, made success impossible.

No practical compromise between balloons and flying machines exists, and no gradual transition from the utilization of the buoyancy of light gases to the lift produced by wing-beats can assist us; we must take a leap from aerostatics back to dynamical aviation.

The balloon, of course, has its own sphere of usefulness, if only as an elevated observation post in its captive form, or to allow itself to be wafted along by the wind. The aims of the science of aviation are totally different. Aerial invention can only be of use to us when we are able to travel through the air rapidly and safely in whatever direction we desire, and not only in the direction in which the wind blows.

The attainment of this aim has suffered a set-back by the balloon, but this contrary influence must cease, and we shall have to apply ourselves most seriously to the solution of the many problems which are still confronting us.

The engineers will then come to some agreement and will give up their indifferent attitude. The interest in active flight is undoubtedly increasing, and, considering the time propitious, we have ventured to publish our experiences on this subject.

§ XL.—Calculation of the Work required for Flight.

We will now calculate for a large bird the work necessary for its flight, basing our calculations upon the experiments which we have described in the previous sections. This will give us an example for the practical employment of the air pressures relating to structures in the form of birds' wings, the publication of these results being one of the many objects of this work.

With regard to the diagrams, we may mention that in our experiments special care was given to the determination of the resistances for the smaller angles; in the neighbourhood of 0° we took observations at intervals of $1\frac{1}{2}$°.

We do not refer to stationary flight in calm air; this we have already dealt with in § XVIII. The stork, which we take as our example, is not capable of such flight, and we do not think that human beings will ever apply this type of flight.

What we propose to investigate is the air pressure during sailing flight, and the effort necessary for forward flight, and for both these types of flight we have only small angles between the direction of flight and the inclination of the wings.

We have selected, as an example, the stork because no other bird of similar size and similar skill in flight gives us such opportunities for observation.

The wing, Fig. 1 on Plate VIII., is that of a white stork, whom we kept for our experiments, whilst the middle, Fig. 44, on page 62, relates to the wings of a black stork; the latter has eight pinions on each wing, but the white stork, to which the following calculations refer, has only six.

The outline of the wing has been obtained by spreading out the wing of a living bird, and then reducing it to $\frac{1}{6}$ actual size for use on Plate VIII. The stork itself weighed 4 kg., and the total area of its two wings was 0·5 sq. m.

What amount of wind is required to enable this stork to sail without beating the wings, *i.e.* so that the spread wings produce so much lifting effect that the stork does not fall?

According to Plate V., a suitably curved wing surface, which is placed horizontally in the wind, is subject to an upward directed air pressure equal to 0·55 of that air pressure which would act on a plane and equal area, with the wind impinging upon it at right angles; this air pressure in the present instance must equal the weight of the bird, namely, 4 kg. Denoting the wind velocity which we wish to calculate by v, then we have the equation—

$$4 = 0{\cdot}55 \times 0{\cdot}13 \times 0{\cdot}5v^2$$

from which $v = 10{\cdot}6$.

That is to say, the stork can "sail" at a wind velocity of 10·6 m., provided its wings are equal in quality to our test surfaces; but since the living wing is obviously better, we may round off the above velocity to 10 m. As already mentioned in § XXXVII., the conditions which obtain for the actual bird's wing must be still more favourable, because the air pressure also contains a small propelling component which is not only sufficient to counteract the wind pressure on the body of the stork, but which even propels that body against the wind. We have observed some storks, which, without wing-beat, without falling, and without circling, flew with a velocity of at least 10 m. against a wind of equal velocity, so that the resistance opposed to the body corresponded to a wind of 20 m. velocity.

The stork at rest, with the wings folded close to the body, and with the feathers fairly loose, has a cross-section of the body (by measurement) of 0·032 sq. m.; but an enormous difference takes place in his shape when the bird spreads the wings, and when the feathers adhere smoothly to the body. In this condition the stork flying forward, with the neck, bill, and legs stretched out, has the appearance of a slender stick between powerful wings.

The cross - section of the body in this position is only 0·008 sq. m., a cross-section which is tapering forwards and backwards (by means of the bill and the tail), so that this favourable shape will introduce a reduction coefficient of $\frac{1}{4}$, and the resulting resistance of the body in the flight direction would be—

$$W = \tfrac{1}{4} \times 0{\cdot}13 \times 0{\cdot}008 \times 20^2 = 0{\cdot}104 \text{ kg.}$$

When the stork sails against the wind with an absolute velocity of 10 m., the pressure below its wings pulls it forward with about 0·1 kg.; the retarding component of the wind pressure being 4 kg., and the propelling component 0·1 kg., the angle between the wind pressure and the perpendicular will have to be arc tang. $\tfrac{1}{40} = 1{\cdot}5°$ approx.

The stork is, however, not compelled to sail exactly against the wind, because the upward component of the wind velocity acts in every direction, and gives up its momentum for perfect sailing flight as long as he moves through the surrounding air with a speed of about 10 m. We have seen that the upward wind pressure which makes sailing flight possible is not always constant but, on the contrary, constantly varies (see Fig. 3, Plate V.).

It is to be assumed that these variations do not cease at 10 m. altitude (the limit to which our observations reached), but that they extend to altitudes in which the birds execute their sailing flight. This is the reason why sailing birds constantly turn and move their wings, trying every instant a new favourable position, and constantly adapting their own velocity to that of the wind. It is probable that the "circling" of birds depends as much upon the periods of wind inclination and wind velocity as upon the increase of wind velocity towards greater altitudes.

It is not to be wondered at that birds are able to perceive the slightest variations in the movement of the air, because the whole of their body surface acts as an organ for this sensation; the long and widely extended wings constitute a sensitive feeling lever, and minute sensibility will be particularly concentrated in the follicles, from which the feathers issue, just as is the case with our finger tips.

In actual "sailing," the flight work itself is, theoretically, nil ; skill is the principal consideration.

Should it ever become possible for man to imitate the splendid sailing movements of birds, he will not require to use steam engines or electro-motors for the purpose; a light, properly shaped and sufficiently movable wing, and the necessary practice in their manipulation, is all that will be required of him. He should unconsciously be able to draw the greatest advantages from whatever wind may be blowing, by properly presenting the wings.

Possibly this requires less skill than some of the tricks practised by artists on the tight rope, at least such skill would not be badly applied, and the risk which attends such experiments would not be greater, especially when starting with small wing surfaces and gradually employing larger ones.

Our rope artists are sometimes not quite inexperienced in the advantages which air resistance introduces. Some years ago I witnessed a performance of a lady artist on a wire rope, during which she constantly fanned herself with a gigantic fan. Of course the object was to create the impression that the introduction of this fan made the performance more difficult; but those who have studied the utilization of air pressures could very well appreciate how the graceful manipulation of this fan was employed by the lady, in order to constantly produce an invisible lateral support by means of the air pressure thus generated, and so to assist the maintenance of equilibrium.

Reverting to our bird example: if the wind does not reach a velocity of 10 m., and if it is impossible for the bird to sail without effort by means of skilful circling and turning, then recourse must be had to wing-beats, and the muscular force must supplement the force of the wind in order to produce artificially the lifting air pressure.

Let us now take an extreme case, as, for example, when the wind renders no assistance whatsoever, but when the stork has to depend entirely upon the effect of its wing-beats. The values of the air pressure which apply to this case are given in Plate VI.

The whole process of flight is now altered, the lifting pressure being divided into two unequal parts, one of which acts during the upstroke of the wing, and the other during the downstroke.

It would be useless to develop a general equation for this kind of flight, because the values of the air pressure which exist under these conditions cannot be expressed by formula, and because there are obviously many different methods of attaining good results.

We have seen how varied may be the function of the upstroke, and how several of these methods may be turned to advantage, if only the downstroke of the wings is suitably carried out; the desired velocity also will determine the actual mode of moving the wings.

Let us consider the special case in which the stork flies in calm air. The following factors must then be considered in the calculation :—

1. The flight velocity.
2. The number of wing-beats per second.
3. The time ratio between the upstroke and downstroke.
4. The amplitude of the wing movement.
5. The inclination of the several sections of the wing with respect to their relative absolute path.

The four first factors can be ascertained, approximately, by simple observation; the fifth factor cannot even be determined from instantaneous photographs, and it is advisable to deduct the most favourable inclinations of the wing by means of tentative calculations.

Foremost in importance is the determination of that case which requires a minimum of motive effort, and we may assume that under ordinary conditions the stork will choose such methods as will reduce the work to minimum. We will assume that flight velocity which will not particularly increase the work to be done. We know that stationary flight requires so much exertion that the stork is incapable of it; that with increased flight velocity the work at first diminishes, but after a certain velocity has been reached the work again increases, since the effort necessary to traverse the air increases with the cube of the velocity. It is obvious that the minimum of the necessary work must be found at some medium velocity, or, another probability, that the work required for widely different velocities must be very near this minimum value.

During a calm, the stork develops a velocity of from 10 to 12 metres per second, because he is able to keep pace with fairly rapid passenger trains; the number of double wing-beats per second is two, and in the case of such a comparatively slow movement it is possible to determine the time ratio of the upstroke and down-stroke by simple observation. It is safe to assume that this ratio is as $2:3$, *i.e.* $\frac{2}{5}$ of the time of a double beat is utilized for the upstroke, and $\frac{3}{5}$ for the downstroke.

The fourth factor—namely, the amplitude of the wing-beat—cannot be expressed in terms of a simple angle, because the unequal movements of the various parts of the wing, as set forth in § XXX., apply to the stork as well as to the gull. Here photography would render good service, and would enable us to check whether the movement upon which wo base our calculations (Fig. 2 on Plate VIII.) is correctly drawn. This Fig. 2 has been drawn by watching the stork either from the front or from the back whilst in full flight.

We have now to inquire whether it is possible, on the strength of the known effects of air pressures, to prove that the stork can sustain flight by means of its wing beats, and how much work is required. For this purpose we imagine the wing (Fig. 1, Plate VIII.) divided into four parts. A is the part which belongs to the upper arm, and B that belonging to the forearm; C is the closed portion of the wing, and D are the areas of the pinions. The dimensions of these several parts as well as their respective areas are noted in the illustration.

Let us assume that each part, A, B, C, D, has a uniform velocity, and that the specific resistance of the centres, a, b, c, d, be uniformly distributed over the respective areas. Fig. 2 illustrates the wing excursion with the amplitudes of a, b, c, d in $\frac{1}{20}$ actual size.

The up and down movement of the wings will be accompanied by a compensating and oppositely directed lifting and falling of the body of the stork; but since the upstroke of the wing also assists in the lifting effort, we need not consider the up and down movement of the body. The upper arm being short, and executing but a moderate movement, the centre of the oscillation for both sides of the stork will be situated somewhere near point a, and the area A describes therefore approximately a straight and, in the present case, a horizontal path.

The excursion of b is taken to equal 0·12 m., that of point c 0·44 m., and that of point d equal to 0·88 m. measured along the arc.

When the stork distributes two wing-beats in one second over a distance of 10 m., he advances 5 m., with one double wing-beat, namely, 2 m. on the upstroke and 3 m. on the downstroke. Marking off these distances, side by side, on a scale of 1 : 50, and taking from Fig. 2, properly reduced, the excursions of the several wing portions, we obtain in Fig. 3, Plate VIII., the absolute paths described by a, b, c, d.; the dotted line is the path of the wing tips.

We have now to determine the inclinations of the wing elements against their absolute paths, and then to find that particular case in which the resistances enable the stork to fly with a minimum of effort.

The quickest way to do this is to calculate for the parts, A, B, C, and D, for upstroke and downstroke, and for a number of acute angles above and below zero, the lifting and propelling components of the resistances and to tabulate the results ; this will give us the necessary knowledge that will enable us to select the best angles.

Let us take, as an example, part C of the wing, on the down-stroke, for an inclination of 3° with its path. The area of C is 0·076 sq. m., and from Plate VII. the proper coefficient for 3° is 0·55 ; the velocity is increased to 10·1 m. (owing to the obliquity of the path), and the air pressure will be—

$$0·55 \times 0·13 \times 0·076 \times 10·1^2 = 0·554 \text{ kg.}$$

The direction of this pressure is shown in Plate VI., and according to Fig. 1 would be directed 3° backwards ; since C is moving down-wards 8½°, the true direction of the air pressure is consequently $8\frac{1}{2} - 3 = 5\frac{1}{2}°$ forward (see Fig. 5, Plate VIII.).

The components are therefore—

Lifting $0·554 \times \cos 5\frac{1}{2}° = 0·551$ kg.
Propelling $0·554 \times \sin 5\frac{1}{2}° = 0·053$ kg.

In a similar manner the two tables, now following, have been calculated, the figures denoting the components in kg. for the respective angles of inclination. The propelling horizontal components have been marked positive (+), the retarding ones negative (−).

UPSTROKE.

Incli- nation.	Portion A.		Portion B.		Portion C.		Portion D.	
	Vertical.	Horizontal.	Vertical.	Horizontal.	Vertical.	Horizontal.	Vertical.	Horizontal.
+ 9°	0·634	− 0·066						
+ 6°	0·555	− 0·044	0·610	− 0·079				
+ 3°	0·436	− 0·023	0·479	− 0·049	0 523	− 0·145		
0°	0·317	− 0·019	0·348	− 0·040	0·395	− 0·112	0·260	− 0·130
− 3°	—	—	0·216	− 0·034	0·235	− 0·077	0·155	− 0·089
− 6°	—	—	—	—	0·135	− 0·070	0·064	− 0·052
− 9°	—	—	—	—	—	—	0·015	0·025
On account of beating motion and shortening					× 1·0		× 1·0	

DOWNSTROKE.

Incli- nation.	Portion A.		Portion B.		Portion C.		Portion D.	
	Vertical.	Horizontal.	Vertical.	Horizontal.	Vertical.	Horizontal.	Vertical.	Horizontal.
+ 9°	0·634	− 0·066	0·690	− 0·048	0·808	+ 0·026	0·504	+ 0·086
+ 6°	0·555	− 0·044	0·610	− 0·024	0·707	+ 0·044	0·442	+ 0·088
+ 3°	0·436	− 0·023	0·479	− 0·008	0·551	+ 0·053	0·350	+ 0 082
0°	0·317	− 0·019	0·348	− 0·010	0·404	+ 0·034	0·260	+ 0 000
− 3°	—	—	0·210	− 0·010	0·252	+ 0·008	0·180	0·030
− 6°	—	—	—	—	0·150	− 0·025	0·078	− 0·001
− 9°	—	—	—	—	—	—	0·011	− 0·037
On account of beating motion					× 1·75		× 2·25	

A good proportion is, for instance, that in which, for the up-stroke, A has an inclination of + 3°, B of 0°, C of − 3°, and D of − 9°, and for the downstroke + 6°, + 6°, + 3°, and 0° relatively, and these values are printed in heavier type in the tables. For the portions C and D the increase of the resistance due to the beating movement cannot be neglected, but since during the up-stroke the wings are somewhat contracted and shortened, the values of the table are not altered, although for the downstroke they should be multiplied by 1·75 and 2·25 respectively.

Under these conditions we obtain the following totals for each wing :—

UPSTROKE.				DOWNSTROKE.		
Portion.	Vertical.	Horizontal.		Portion.	Vertical.	Horizontal.
A	0·436	− 0·023		A	0·555	− 0·044
B	0·348	− 0·040		B	0·610	− 0·024
C	0·235	− 0·077		C	0·964	+ 0·093
D	− 0·015	− 0·035		D	0·585	+ 0·135
Kg. . . .	1·004	− 0·175		Kg. . . .	2·714	+ 0·160

And for both wings—

Kg. . . .	2·008	− 0·350		Kg. . . .	5·428	+ 0·320

Deducting the lifting pressure during the upstroke from the weight of the bird, 4 − 2·008, leaves 1·992 kg. for the weight which forces the stork downwards during the period of upstroke.

On page 110 we have seen that the resistance due to the body of the stork is 0·1 kg. when the velocity is 20 m., thus for 10 m. it amounts to about 0·025 kg. This must be added to the restraining component during the upstroke, so that the total retarding force is 0·350 + 0·025 = 0·375 kg. The stork is therefore subject, during the wing upstroke, to a downward pressing force of 1·992 kg., and a retarding force of 0·375 kg.

These have to be compensated by the downstroke, which, since it lasts $\frac{2}{3}$ as long as the upstroke, only requires a lift of $\frac{2}{3} \times 1·992 = 1·328$ kg., and a propelling force of $\frac{2}{3} \times 0·375 = 0·250$ kg. From the lifting air pressure during the downstroke we have to deduct the weight of the bird, and from the propelling force the body resistance. Therefore—

$$\text{Lift} \qquad\qquad 5·428 − 4 \qquad = 0·295 \text{ kg.}$$
$$\text{Propelling force} \quad 0·320 − 0·025 = 0·295 \text{ kg.}$$

Both of which are in excess of what is required, so that the stork is able to fly horizontally in calm air.

We have drawn in Figs. 4 and 5, on Plate VIII., the above calculated wing pressures both for upstroke and downstroke to the proper scale, giving the inclinations of the profiles and the directions of the path for the corresponding positions. The section of the pinions is drawn actual size and with the actual inclination.

A stork is, however, able to fly under many other conditions of wing inclinations, but the above example represents approximately the minimum of work.

No work is done by the stork during the upstroke of the wings, since these simply yield to the pressure acting from below. If the wing could be bent upward in its joints, during this phase, *i.e.* somewhat like an elastic spring, so that it were able to assist the downward pull of the tendons and muscles during the down-stroke, then it might even be possible to store some *work* in this way; to a certain degree this really applies to the natural wing. This work is determined by multiplying the lifting pressures with their respective paths.

We have for the upstroke—

For area A . . .	Work	$0 \cdot 0$		
„ B . . .	„	$0 \cdot 348 \times 0 \cdot 12 =$	$0 \cdot 0417$ kgm.
„ C . . .	„	$0 \cdot 235 \times 0 \cdot 44 =$	$0 \cdot 1034$ „
„ D . . .	„	$- 0 \cdot 015 \times 0 \cdot 88 =$	$- 0 \cdot 0132$ „

For the whole wing . . . $+ 0 \cdot 1319$ „

Theoretically, the gain in work for both wings and for one upstroke would be $2 \times 0 \cdot 1319 = 0 \cdot 2638$ kg., or per second $2 \times 0 \cdot 2638 = 0 \cdot 5276$ kg.

For the downstroke the amounts of work are—

For area A . . .	Work	$0 \cdot 0$		
„ B . . .	„	$0 \cdot 610 \times 0 \cdot 12 =$	$0 \cdot 0732$ kgm.
„ C . . .	„	$0 \cdot 964 \times 0 \cdot 44 =$	$0 \cdot 4241$ „
„ D . . .	„	$0 \cdot 585 \times 0 \cdot 88 =$	$0 \cdot 5148$ „

For the whole wing . . . $1 \cdot 0121$ „

Thus for both wings $2 \cdot 0242$ kgm., and per second $4 \cdot 04$ kgm.

If we deduct a small part of the theoretical gain of work, as before explained, we may round off the work done by the stork in forward flight and in calm air to 4 kgm.

Still somewhat more favourable will be the result, when the movement of the arm portion is less, such as indicated by a dotted line in Fig. 2 on Plate VIII., *i.e.* if point *b* moves only $0 \cdot 06$ m., *c* only $0 \cdot 26$ m., but *d* $0 \cdot 76$ m. For these conditions we calculate the following tables :—

UPSTROKE.

Incli-nation.	Portion A.		Portion B.		Portion C.		Portion D.	
	Vertical.	Horizontal.	Vertical.	Horizontal.	Vertical.	Horizontal.	Vertical.	Horizontal.
+ 9°	0·634	− 0·066						
+ 6°	0·555	− 0·042	0·610	− 0·063				
+ 3°	**0·436**	**− 0·023**	**0·479**	**− 0·037**	0·560	− 0·102		
0	0·317	− 0·019	0·348	− 0·030	0·408	− 0·087	0·240	− 0·105
− 3°	—	—	0·216	− 0·028	**0·250**	**− 0·059**	0·148	− 0·072
− 6°	—	—	—	—	0·131	− 0·057	**0·072**	**− 0·055**
− 9°	—	—	—	—	—	—	−0·016	− 0·042
By reason of the beating action and con-traction . . . . }					× 1·0		× 1·0	

DOWNSTROKE.

Incli-nation.	Portion A.		Portion B.		Portion C.		Portion D.	
	Vertical.	Horizontal.	Vertical.	Horizontal.	Vertical.	Horizontal.	Vertical.	Horizontal.
+ 9°	0·634	− 0·066	0·690	− 0·060	0·808	− 0·014	0·505	0·071
+ 6°	0·555	− 0·042	0·610	− 0·036	0·707	+ 0·006	0·442	0·077
+ 3°	**0·436**	**− 0·023**	**0·479**	**− 0·017**	**0·555**	**+ 0·019**	**0·346**	**0·069**
0°	0·317	− 0·019	0·348	− 0·015	0·404	+ 0·010	0·250	0·048
− 3°	—	—	0·216	− 0·019	0·252	− 0·003	0·132	0·020
By reason of the beating action					× 1·55		× 2·15	

Selecting the following surface inclinations—

Upstroke   A + 3°, B + 3°, C − 3°, D − 6°,

Downstroke A + 3°, B + 0°, C + 3°, D + 3°,

we obtain the total pressures—

UPSTROKE.				DOWNSTROKE.		
Portion.	Vertical.	Horizontal.		Portion.	Vertical.	Horizontal.
A	0·436	− 0·023		A	0·436	− 0·023
B. . . .	0·479	− 0·037		B. . . .	0·479	− 0·017
C. . . .	0·250	− 0·059		C. . . .	0·860	+ 0·029
D. . . .	0·072	− 0·055		D. . . .	0·744	+ 0·148
Kg. . . .	1·237	− 0·174		Kg. . . .	2·519	+ 0·137

Thus for both wings—

Kg. . . .	2·474	− 0·348		Kg. . . .	5·038	+ 0·274

The stork is pressed down by its weight and retarded by its body resistance during the upstroke with—

1·526 kg. and 0·373 kg. respectively.

So that the downstroke must furnish—

$$\tfrac{2}{3} \times 1\text{·}526 = 1\text{·}017 \text{ kg. lifting force.}$$
$$\tfrac{2}{3} \times 0\text{·}373 = 0\text{·}248 \text{ kg. tractive force.}$$

In reality it yields—

$$5\text{·}038 - 4 \qquad = 1\text{·}038 \text{ kg. lifting force.}$$
$$0\text{·}274 - 0\text{·}025 = 0\text{·}249 \text{ kg. tractive force.}$$

The theoretical gain of work during upstroke would be—

For A	. . . . .	0·0
„ B	. . . . .	0·479 × 0·06 = 0·0287 kgm.
„ C	. . . . .	0·250 × 0·26 = 0·0650 „
„ D	. . . . .	0·072 × 0·76 = 0·0547 „
	For the whole wing . . .	0·1484 „

The work used up in the downstroke is—

For A	. . . . .	0·0
„ B	. . . . .	0·479 × 0·06 = 0·0287 kgm.
„ C	. . . . .	0·860 × 0·26 = 0·2236 „
„ D	. . . . .	0·744 × 0·76 = 0·5654 „
	For the total wing . . .	0·8177 „

The work for the down-beat per second is now $4 \times 0\text{·}8177 = 3\text{·}2708$ kgm. whilst we save theoretically $4 \times 0\text{·}1484 = 0\text{·}5436$ kgm. during the upstroke.

Taking only a small portion of this saving into consideration, we can place the work necessary for this type of flight at 3·2 kgm., *i.e.* somewhat less than for the preceding example with stronger wing movement.

The retarding effect during the upstroke, due to the wing-tips, may be further diminished—and actual birdflight proves it—by letting the extreme wing portions describe an upward curved path, corresponding to the curvature of the wing. If we apply this method to the parts C and D, the work is reduced to 2·7 kgm.

These calculations allow us to gain an insight into the various factors which make it possible to economize in work during forward flight; the minimum is attained when the greater part of the wing passes horizontally, with the best inclination, through the air and when the wing-tips, by their large movement, produce a tractive effect.

The limiting condition would be present, when the whole surface were immovable, but pushed forward by means of a special propeller. To make the work a minimum, the surface should be given that inclination which ensures the smallest retarding component which, according to Plate VI., is + 3°.

For such a surface, horizontally moved, the air pressure would enclose an angle of 3° with the perpendicular, and, for one capable of just sustaining its weight G, the horizontal retarding component would be $G \times \tan 3°$. To overcome this force, with the velocity v, the propelling work would have to be—

$$v G \tan 3° = 0.0524 v G,$$

and this would represent the only work required for flight.

Velocity v depends upon the area of the supporting surface. Taking into account the reduction factor for 3° (according to Plate VII., 0.55), we have—

$$G = 0.55 \times 0.13\,F v^2 \text{ and } v = 3.74 \sqrt{\frac{G}{F}}$$

For the stork the ratio $\dfrac{G}{F} = 8$, and consequently $v = 10.58$.

The work, as above stated, would be $0.0524 \times 10.58 \times G = 0.55G$. Assuming, for the moment, that we have a propeller of negligible weight, with an efficiency of 100 per cent., then for a body weighing 4 kg. (the stork), the requisite work would only amount to $0.55 \times 4 = 2.2$ kgm.

The foregoing calculations demonstrate that we have approached this theoretical minimum very closely, and we are therefore justified in concluding that not many better forms of movement for flight in calm air exist.

Any further advantage can only be imagined to result from the better direction and better utilization of the air pressure due to a further improvement of the wing shape.

On page 88, when studying "sailing" flight, we have seen that the air pressures upon birds' wings have a more forward direction than we were able to demonstrate, and we were forced to conclude that for small angles of incidence the pressures were $1\frac{1}{2}°$ in advance of those shown. In the case of an inclination of 3°, the resistance would only lag 1½° behind the perpendicular, thus reducing the retarding component by half and consequently the flight work to 1·35 kgm. It is likewise possible that the profile of the wing, in its longitudinal direction, contributes to the saving of work both in sailing flight and in forward flight.

For the investigation of this possible effect, as well as the effect of beating motion during forward flight, we should have to construct a test apparatus of the exact shape and movement of birds, in order to discover, by actual practice, the last and minute differences in the effects of air pressures.

In order to apply the results of our calculations for the stork to a flying apparatus for human beings, we may assume the weight of the latter to be twenty times that of a stork. In calm air this work would be 20 × 1·35 = 27 kgm., or 0·36 h.p., provided the area was 10 sq. m. and that all the favourable factors of bird-flight were introduced. Why should this not become possible, why may we not acquire the art of constructing and the skill of managing apparatus which closely approaches the perfection of a bird's flying apparatus ?

In § XXXV. we calculated the work for human flight in calm air as 0·3 h.p., but since this applied to a larger sustaining area, and because we then neglected the resistances due to the wing upstroke, that calculation was only of theoretical interest, whilst in the last numerical example we have considered all the actual imperfections and contrary influences.

Work of this magnitude might be temporarily exerted by man, but however interesting it might be, such kind of flight would be of little practical value.

Increasing the area of the wings would not result in any improvement, and we may therefore assert that muscular effort will not enable man to fly for any length of time.

To render flight in calm air practically possible, we should have to utilize light motors.

Fortunately for the art of flight, however, the occurrence of calms is rare. This condition, which to the balloonist who wishes to steer his apparatus is so essential, is quite the exception in the upper strata of the air, and, speaking generally, we must consider the wind and not the absence of wind in our calculations.

All the various magnitudes of work necessary for wind velocities between 0 and 10 m. lie within the limits, which we have determined in the preceding paragraphs.

The ascending direction of the wind for all wind velocities remains practically constant, so that the momentum, imparted to the flyer and which reduces the requisite work, is proportional to the square of the wind velocity. Hence this reduction amounts to—

For a velocity of . .	1 m.	2 m.	3 m.	4 m.	5 m.	6 m.	7 m.	8 m.	9 m.
	0·01	0·04	0·09	0·16	0·25	0·36	0·49	0·64	0·81

of the work.

We have determined the minimum work for calm air to be 27 kgm. for a velocity of 10 m., and the above figures therefore reduce the work to—

Wind velocity . .	1 m.	2 m.	3 m.	4 m.	5 m.	6 m.	7 m.	8 m.	9 m.
Kgm.	26·7	25·9	24·6	22·7	20·3	17·3	13·8	9·7	5·1

From these results it appears that when the wind velocity lies between 6 m. and 9 m., i.e. for a " fresh " wind, the work required for flight becomes so moderate that even if some of the conditions of flight are much less favourable than we at first assumed, it will be quite feasible for man to operate a suitable apparatus by his muscular effort only.

§ XLI.—The Construction of Flying Apparatus.

The last section gave us the calculations for the relation between the work necessary for flight and the resulting effect. Extending the conditions on a suitable scale, we must obtain the shapes and dimensions of such apparatus which would serve for human flight.

It is not our object to create sensational impressions, and we leave it to the imagination of our readers to form their opinions as to what man would look like during flight under the above developed considerations. We will, however, shortly recapitulate the fundamental points from which the construction of flying apparatus would have to be evolved, when the experimental results set down in this volume are accepted as a basis for the design.

1st.—The design of practical flying machines is not absolutely dependent upon the provision of powerful and light motors.

2nd.—Hovering flight in calm air does not come within the scope of human flight by muscular exertion, this kind of flight requires under the most favourable conditions at least 1·5 h.p. Forward flight, in calm air, with a minimum velocity of 10 m, may be possible to man, but for a short time only, as it requires 0·27 h.p.

3rd.—With a wind of mean velocity, the muscular power of man is sufficient to move a suitable flying apparatus, provided a sufficient speed of flight is maintained.

4th.—When the velocity of the wind is above 10 m., sailing flight without muscular effort will be possible for man, provided he uses suitable supporting surfaces.

5th.—Any flying apparatus which will be effective and requiring only a minimum of work must conform in shape and properties with the wings of large and good flying birds.

6th.—For every kilogram of total weight, the supporting area must measure from $\frac{1}{10}$ to $\frac{1}{8}$ sq. m.

7th.—It is possible to construct a practical apparatus with an area of 10 sq. m. and a weight of about 15 kg., employing willow canes and some textile covering.

8th.—The flight area per kilogram of a human being mounted on such an apparatus, and weighing altogether 90 kg., would be $\frac{1}{9}$ sq. m., a figure which corresponds approximately to that applying to the larger birds.

9th.—It will be a matter of experiment to determine whether the broad shape of wing with resolved pinions, such as we see in birds of prey, or the long pointed shape of wing of the sea birds, are preferable.

10th.—In the former case the dimensions of the wing would be 8 m. span, and 1·6 m. greatest width. (See Fig. 88.)

11th.—When employing the slender wing shape, the corre-

sponding dimensions would be 11 m. span, and 1·4 m. greatest
width. (See Fig. 89.)

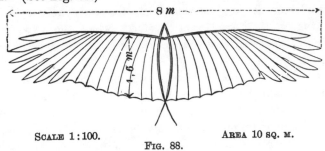

SCALE 1 : 100.   AREA 10 SQ. M.

FIG. 88.

12th.—It is of secondary importance for the support afforded,
whether a tail is fitted or not.

13th.—The wing must show a curvature on the underside.

14th.—The camber of the curvature should be about $\frac{1}{12}$ of the
width of the wing, in accordance with the construction of a bird's
wing.

15th.—Experiments will show whether in the case of larger
areas weaker or stronger curvatures offer greater advantage.

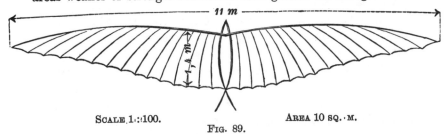

SCALE 1 : 100.   AREA 10 SQ. M.

FIG. 89.

16th.—The ribs and stiffenings of the wings should be fitted
near the leading edge.

17th.—Whenever possible, this thickened edge should be
provided with a tapering edge in front.

18th.—The geometrical shape of the curvature should be a
parabola, more curved towards the leading edge and getting
straighter towards the back.

19th.—For larger areas the best shape of the curve would
have to be established by experiment, and that shape, the pressures
upon which for small angles of inclination are most nearly in the
direction of movement, should be preferred.

20th.—The design must be such that the wing may rotate around its longitudinal axis, a rotation which is effected wholly or partly by the air pressure itself; this rotation should be strongest towards the wing-tips.

21st.—In ordinary forward flight the broader wing portions near the body are moved as little as possible and act chiefly as supporting surfaces.

22nd.—The forward traction which is to maintain the flight velocity is produced by the wing-tips or pinions, which are beaten down with the leading edge inclined downwards.

23rd.—The broader wing parts should act as supporting surfaces also during the upstroke.

24th.—The wing-tips should experience a minimum of resistance during the upstroke.

25th.—The downstroke should occupy at least $\frac{6}{10}$ of the time necessary for a complete double beat.

26th.—Only the end portion of the wings should take part in the up and down stroke, the supporting wing portions remaining immovable as in sailing flight.

27th.—The up and down movements of the wing-tips must not take place by means of a joint, or the wing shape will be deformed; the excursion of the tips must, on the contrary, merge gradually into the comparative immovability of the other wing portions.

28th.—Wing-beats which are executed by human muscular power should be effected by means of the legs, not simultaneously but alternately, so that every down-push of the legs produces a double beat.

29th.—The upstroke might be effected by the air pressure itself.

30th.—It would be of advantage to store the effect of air pressure during the upstroke (by means of springs or otherwise) so that it may be utilized again during the down-beat, and thus save work.

These would be some of the chief considerations.

But from our own experience we are sure that no one would imagine the lifting effect of the wind to be of such magnitude, as he will actually experience when placed in the wind with such wings.

Human muscular effort is insufficient to operate such wings in a wind without previous training, and in all probability the first result with such an apparatus, although it may be well calculated but lightly built, would be its total wreckage after the very first strong gust of wind.

For this reason we think it necessary to develop a special sense for such wind effects, and at first to practice the safe manipulation of such wings on a smaller scale. Only when we have learned how to act on air and wind by means of suitable surfaces—that is, after this has become almost intuitive—may we venture upon a real flight. With this warning we will conclude this section.

It will be left to the skill of the designer to give practical value to the above developed principles of flight by constructing and developing practical wings and supporting surfaces.

If at any future time we should have collected sufficient new material relating to such improvements, we may perhaps again publish our results.

§ XLII.—Concluding Remarks.

Looking back upon the preceding sections, a number of experimental results stand out, which have a direct bearing upon the solution of the problem of flight, because they refer to the several factors which together make up the effort necessary for flight.

An understanding of the most elementary conceptions of dynamics is all that we require in order to prove the correctness of these results, and it is fortunate that the most important features of flight are of a very simple dynamical character, embodying only the theory of the equilibrium—and of the parallelogram of force.

Yet, the literature of flight demonstrates with what facility errors and wrong conclusions are apt to creep into such dynamical treatment of the subject, and this fact caused us to analyse the dynamics of flight in as elementary a manner as possible.

In this way the treatment of a somewhat awkward subject has been greatly facilitated, and the author also entertains the hope that not only the science of aviation but also that of dynamics, her indispensable handmaid, may gain new adherents, stimulating some of his readers to gain a closer insight into the teachings of theoretical mechanics, or least to refresh his college teaching.

The study of aviation requires a different treatment than other technical subjects, and the peculiar circle of students to whom it appeals secures it a separate position. No clergyman, officer, medical man, philologist, agriculturist, or merchant would think of devoting himself to a specialized study of steam engines, of mining, or of textiles; they are aware that these departments of industrial investigations are in capable hands; but they are all interested in the promotion of flight, every one of these several professions and trades being anxious to assist, and, possibly by a lucky inspiration, to bring nearer the time when man will be able to fly.

The science of flight cannot, as yet, be considered a separate profession, and it does not yet include a series of exponents worthy of absolute confidence; this is due to the existing uncertainty and want of system, no firm basis having been laid down, from which every investigator must start.

This must explain why this volume addresses itself to all, and why, in the first few sections, we have endeavoured to convert the interest in flight, which every person evinces who takes up this work, into an interest in that science, without the knowledge of which a large part of the fascination which attends the investigation of the problem of flight is lost.

Proceeding onwards, we have shown how hopeless would be the position of the flight problem had we to depend upon *plane* surfaces only.

We have demonstrated that even in those cases, when the advantages accruing from curved surfaces are not utilized, *i.e.* when there is no forward flight, the "work" necessary for flight must not be calculated from the ordinary formula for air resistance, but that, in the case of beating wings, there exists another kind of air resistance, which reaches a given magnitude for smaller velocities and requires less work to overcome it.

We were able to adduce very tangible experiments, which prove beyond doubt that beating movements produce an air pressure which is totally different from that produced by the uniform movement of a surface through air.

It was further explained that forward flight by itself could not be the key to the problem of flight, if we retained plane surfaces.

Finally we endeavoured to prove, by actual experiments, that the true secret of birdflight was the curvature of the bird's wing, which accounted for the natural, small effort required for forward flight, and which, together with the peculiar lifting effects of wind, explained the ability of birds to " sail."

All this we found out from natural birdflight, and we shall never be able to utilize these properties of form and movement without emulating birdflight.

We are, therefore, forced to the conclusion that the only possibility of attaining efficient human flight lies in the exact imitation of bird-flight with regard to the aerodynamic conditions, because this is probably the sole method which permits of free, rapid flight, with a minimum of effort.

Possibly, the views which we have expressed in this volume may be of help in directing the flight problem into another and secure groove, thus forming a foundation upon which a real system may be erected which shall lead to the desired goal. The fundamental idea of free flight, which is now established beyond question, is as follows: the bird flies because it is able to act on the surrounding air in a suitable way, by means of suitably shaped wings.

How to construct such wings, and how to move them, are the two main problems of the art of flight.

An observation of the manner in which Nature has solved these problems, and the rejection of plane surfaces as unsuitable for the flight of larger creatures, has gradually reduced the threatening dimensions of the barrier, which the provision of the requisite motive power seemed to erect between us and the attainment of human flight. We perceive how the properties of the curved natural wing push the force factor more in the background, and make flight appear more as a question of skill.

Motive power and force are numerically limited, but not so skill. With "force" we are, sooner or later, confronted by permanent impossibilities, but the progress of our skill can only be temporarily checked by difficulties.

Let us observe the gull, which floats almost motionless, three arm-lengths above our head! The sinking sun traces the shadow of the wing edge upon the slightly curved under surface of its wing,

usually light grey in colour, but now a ruddy gold; every rotation
of the wings alters the width of this shadow, which also gives us
an idea of the camber of the wing, when the gull rests on the air.

Such is the material wing, which, in the words of "Faust,"
Goethe had in mind—

> " Aye, 'twill not be so easy,
> To mate the wings of mind with material wings."

It will, indeed, be no easy matter to construct a useful wing
for man, built upon the lines of the natural wing and endowed
with all the dynamically economical properties of the latter; and
it will be even a more difficult task to master the wind, that
erratic force which so often destroys our handiwork, with those
material wings which nature has not made part of our own body.
But we must admit the possibility that continued investigation
and experience will bring us ever nearer to that solemn moment,
when the first man will rise from earth by means of wings, if
only for a few seconds, and marks that historical moment which
heralds the inauguration of a new era in our civilization.

K

Addendum.

GLIDERS AND FLYING MACHINES IN THE LIGHT OF OUR EXPERIMENTS.

THE last few years have witnessed a great spread of gliding flights. Many clubs and societies have been founded to foster the new sport. On the occasion of the Frankfurt Exhibition (Ila), several more or less successful glides took place on suitable days, over the aviation ground, the authorities wisely permitting such flights only during medium winds, and thus preventing accidents.

The great danger attending such glides arises from the fact that the supporting surfaces, especially in the case of monoplanes, rest, as it were, upon the surface of a globe, and are in an unstable equilibrium in every direction, the only safeguard against it being the vertical rudder. It seems advisable to fix such a rudder both before and aft the supporting surfaces, and to couple them together; this would bring about a symmetrical distribution of the air pressure, in case the apparatus acts as parachute during a vertical drop.

Great danger also is introduced by sudden changes in wind direction. The vertical rudder is not capable of bringing the machine into the new wind direction with sufficient rapidity. If the supporting planes are arranged as a dihedral angle, the surface which presents itself to the wind coming obliquely from the front will be considerably lifted, and the opposite plane pressed down, thus making matters worse, and only a rapid, energetic displacement of the centre of gravity can re-establish the disturbed balance.

If it were possible to independently adjust the two halves of the planes, so that they rotate more or less round their longitudinal axis (par. 20, § XLI.), the effect of lateral gusts could be very simply compensated, but the dihedral arrangement of the wings must be abandoned; this reduces the difference between the two planes, and a slight inclination of the leading edge of the windward plane, assisted by a slight upward tilt of the corresponding opposite leading edge, will preserve the equilibrium.

Birds possess a special organ in their wings which enables

FIG. 90.—Last Model of Glider with movable pinions, designed for motive power (without motor).

them to direct the leading edge of the wings, a rudimentary thumb which is independently movable.

We will now consider the effect of the components of air resistance upon gliders and screw-propelled flying machines.

The gliding flights of my late brother were executed under the following conditions :—

The area of the supporting planes was 14 sq. m.; for a wind velocity of 6 m., the velocity of the glider was 5 m., the drop 18 m., and the length of the flight path 300 m. at an inclination of 4°. The total weight of the glider and pilot = 105 kg.

FIG. 91.—Biplane in Flight.

Employing Plate V. we obtain—

For the air resistance $14 \times 11^2 \times 0.52 \times 0.13 = 114$ kg.
The lifting pressure $114 \times \cos 4°$ $= 113$ kg.
The tractive pressure $114 \times \sin 4° = 7.45$ kg.

The areas of pilot and framework were 0.9 sq. m., and offered a resistance of $0.9 \times 11^2 \times 0.5 \times 0.13 = 6.71$ kg.

Total. weight   105 kg.

Surplus of propelling force 0.74 kg.

Surplus of sustaining force   8 kg.

This slight surplus in both directions made it possible to compensate for eventual disturbing influences as regards change of wind direction and variation in the equilibrium.

The brothers Wright started with gliding flights, using the results of our experiments on the lifting properties of curved surfaces. Their leading idea was to utilize this lifting effect in calm air by pushing these surfaces forward through the action of motors and propellers, foregoing the assistance of the wind, and thus attaining security and independence from the erratic changes of wind direction.

A vertical rudder, jutting out far in front, and a horizontal rudder at a considerable distance at the rear, enable them to control the machine even in a light wind. The propellers, which are fitted behind the supporting planes, are driven by a light 26 h.p. motor, and impart to the machine a velocity of between 17 and 20 m.

Under these conditions the disturbing influences of irregular wind directions may be neglected, so long as the wind is moderate, or one may even travel with the wind.

Nevertheless, all aviators of the present day prefer to fly in a perfect calm, since gusty weather often brings about dangerous accidents.

An increase in the

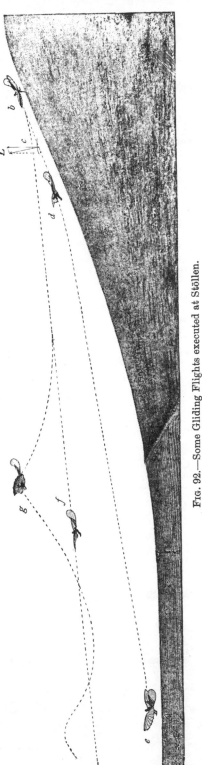

FIG. 92.—Some Gliding Flights executed at Stöllen.

velocity and size of the supporting planes has made it possible to obtain such a lift, that one or two passengers in addition to the pilot could be taken aloft.

Fig. 98.—Gliding Flight at Stöllen.

We will now consider a certain flight carried out by Orville Wright with two passengers.

The aeroplane consists of two supporting planes arranged one above the other, each having an area of 24 sq. m.; the vertical rudder likewise consists of two super-imposed

Fig. 94.—Gliding Flight at Stöllen.

smaller planes, which bring up the total supporting area to 55 sq. m.

The biplanes which we used formerly gave the same supporting effect of an area of 18 sq. m., as did a monoplane with 14 sq. m. area, and we may therefore take the 55 sq. m. of the Wright flyer to be equivalent to a monoplane of $\dfrac{55 \times 14}{18} = 43$ sq. m.

The total weight of the flyer with its three passengers is approximately 580 kg., the average velocity 17 m. The head resistance, which is a most important factor, can only be estimated, as no particulars are given concerning it in any publications dealing with this machine. I therefore assume it to be 1·6 sq. m., and to be composed of the surfaces of the three persons, the motor, and the frame; since these various parts are rounded, we may multiply the above area by 0·5. For a horizontal position of the supporting planes, and using Plate VI. (without the lift due to the wind), we obtain an air pressure—

$$L = 43 \times 17^2 \times 0\text{·}38 \times 0\text{·}13 = 613 \text{ kg.}$$

Since the resulting lifting pressure is inclined 3° backwards the actual lifting pressure is $= 613 \times \cos 3° = 612$ kg.

Deducting the total weight 580 „

leaves a lifting surplus of 32 kg.

The drift will be $613 \times \sin 3° = 31\text{·}8$ kg.
The head resistance $1\text{·}6 \times 0\text{·}5 \times 17^2 \times 0\text{·}13 = 29\text{·}8$ „

Total 61·6 kg.

This retarding force must be overcome by the propellers.

For a velocity of 17 m. the necessary work is—

$$\frac{61\text{·}6 \times 17}{75} = 14 \text{ h.p.}$$

Assuming the efficiency of the propeller to be 60 per cent., we should require a motor of $\dfrac{14}{0\text{·}6} = 23\text{·}3$ h.p.

The Brothers Wright state that their motor was one of 26 h.p., so that in this flyer we still have a slight surplus of supporting and engine-power.

It is due to the arrangement of the propellers behind the supporting planes and to the distance between this and the vertical rudder that the Wright flyers show the peculiar wave motion in their flights. We may compare this to a waggon which is moved backward, the moving force being at the back of the waggon, whilst the shafts are used for steering; it is almost impossible, under these conditions, to move in a straight line for any considerable time.

All designs of flying machines in which the propellers are in front of the planes, and which have the vertical rudder at the back, are free from this wave motion; the traction of the propeller causes the planes to follow in that direction, and no change in the position of the vertical rudder can act instantaneously. But the following considerations will show that this arrangement likewise has its disadvantages.

As an example I select the famous flight of Santos Dumont from St. Cyr to Buc with his minute "Demoiselle."

The areas of this monoplane measure 9·5 sq. m., the velocity 25 m., the weight is stated to be 118 kg., and I estimate the head area, according to the illustrations, to be 0·6 sq. m.

For this example likewise we must employ Plate VI. for the horizontal position of the plane—

$$L = 9·5 \times 25^2 \times 0·38 \times 0·13 = 293 \text{ kg.}$$

This gives a vertical pressure $= 293 \times \cos 3° = 292$ kg.
Deduct the weight 118 „

And we have the very considerable surplus of 174 kg.

The retarding pressure is $293 \times \sin 3°$ $= 15·1$ kg.

The head resistance of the area is somewhat increased because the propeller is in front, and throws air backward with a larger velocity than the relative velocity of the flyer. Increasing the latter by 10 m., we have to use for the calculation 35 m.

The head resistance is therefore—

$$0·6 \times 0·5 \times 35^2 \times 0·13 = 47·7 \text{ kg.}$$

Total 62·8 „

This resistance requires $\dfrac{62·8 \times 25}{75} = 21$ h.p.

Assuming the efficiency of the propeller to be again 60 per cent., the power of the motor must be $\dfrac{21}{0\cdot6} = 35$ h.p.

According to published information, the motor had only an output of 30 h.p.

From this fact, and from the very large surplus of lifting power, I conclude that some other forces must here come into play; and this conclusion is still further strengthened by the fact that we cannot assume the supporting planes to be subject to a uniform air pressure behind the propeller.

I consider that portion of the supporting plane which is directly behind the propeller negligible so far as its lifting effect is concerned.

The following calculation throws further light on this conclusion :—

Reducing the supporting planes by 4·5 sq. m., leaves us 5 sq. m. area.

These give L = $5 \times 25^2 \times 0\cdot38 \times 0\cdot13 = 154$ kg.

The vertical pressure is $154 \times \cos 3°$	= 153 kg.
Deducting the weight	118 „
We have a surplus of	35 kg.

The retarding pressure = $154 \times \sin 3° = 7\cdot8$ kg.

The head resistance as before	47·7 „
Total	55·5 kg.

This resistance requires $\dfrac{55\cdot5 \times 25}{75} = 18$ h.p.

at 60 per cent. deficiency; for the propeller the output of the motor must be $\dfrac{18}{0\cdot6} = 30$ h.p., which corresponds to the actual condition.

A study of other flyers with the propellers arranged in front gives similar results.

The employment of curved surfaces in connection with light explosion motors has produced good results; but it would be a mistake to be satisfied with those results, and to consider that the last word has been spoken on the development of aviation.

As yet, strong winds are the terror of all aviators, and to the whims of the wind have been added the whims of the motor.

We have not yet succeeded in taming the wind and utilizing its wild forces. We have to continue our investigations; experiments guided by theoretical considerations will have to clear up many problems before we can claim victory over the air.

INDEX

THE END

LIST OF PLATES

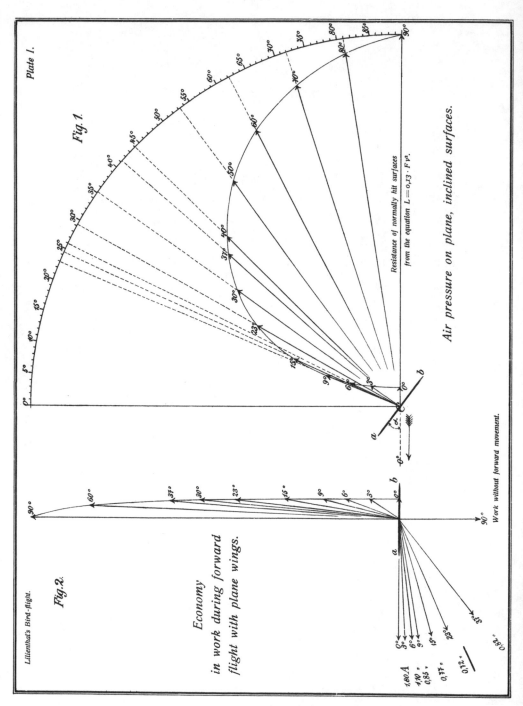

Lilienthal's Bird-flight.

Plate 1.

Fig. 1.

Resistance of normally hit surfaces
from the equation $L = 0{,}13 \cdot F v^2$.

Air pressure on plane, inclined surfaces.

Work without forward movement.

Fig. 2.

Economy
in work during forward
flight with plane wings.

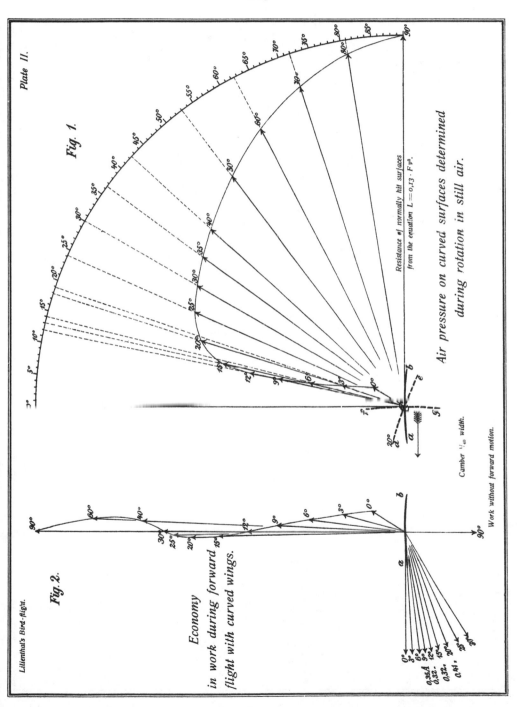

Plate II.

Fig. 1.

Air pressure on curved surfaces determined
during rotation in still air.

Resistance of normally hit surfaces
from the equation $L = o,13 \cdot Fv^2$.

Camber $^{1}/_{40}$ width.

Work without forward motion.

Lilienthal's Bird-flight.

Fig. 2.

Economy
in work during forward
flight with curved wings.

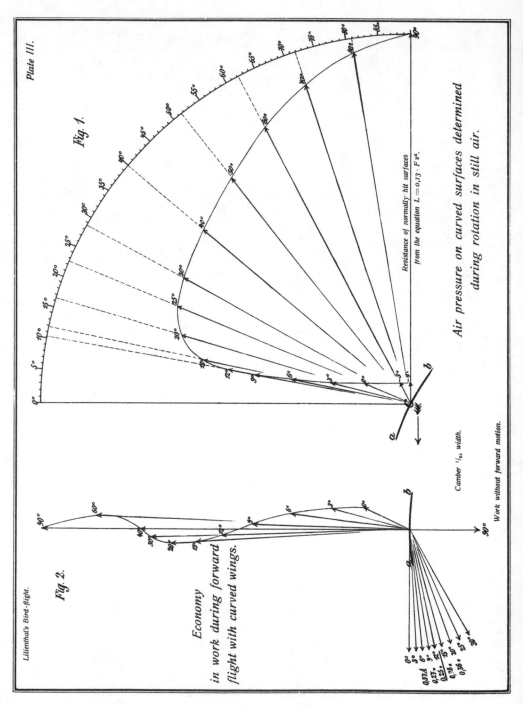

Plate III.

Fig. 1.

Resistance of normally hit surfaces
from the equation L = 0,13 · F v².

Air pressure on curved surfaces determined
during rotation in still air.

Camber ¹/₁₃ width.

Work without forward motion.

Lilienthal's Bird-flight.

Fig. 2.

Economy
in work during forward
flight with curved wings.

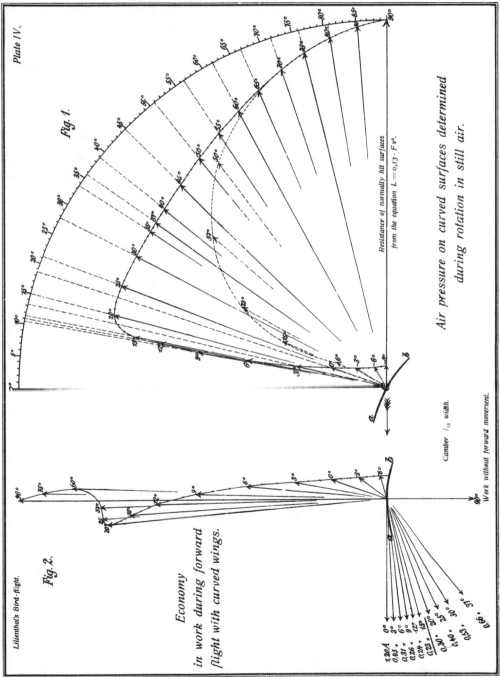

Plate IV.

Fig. 1.

Resistance of normally hit surfaces

from the equation $L = 0,13 \cdot F v^2$.

Air pressure on curved surfaces determined
during rotation in still air.

Camber $^1/_{12}$ width.

Lilienthal's Bird-flight.

Fig. 2.

Economy
in work during forward
flight with curved wings.

Work without forward movement.

148

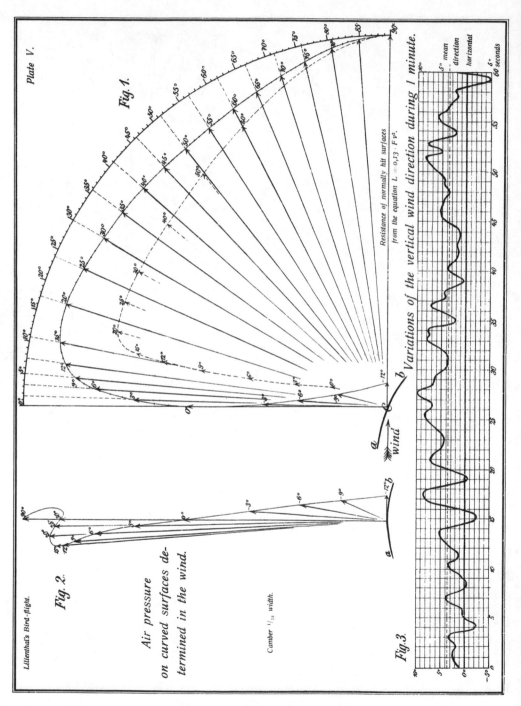

Plate V.

Lilienthal's Bird-flight.

Fig. 2.

Air pressure
on curved surfaces de-
termined in the wind.

Camber ¹/₁₂ width.

Fig. 1.

Resistance of normally hit surfaces
from the equation $L = 0,13 \cdot F \cdot v^2$.

wind

b Variations of the vertical wind direction during 1 minute.

5° mean
direction
horizontal
60 seconds

Fig. 3.

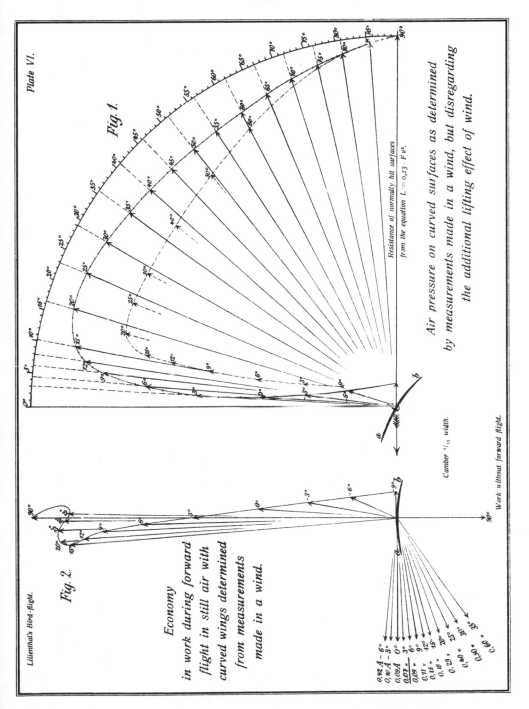

Plate VI.

Fig. 1.

Resistance of normally hit surfaces

from the equation $L = 0,13 \cdot F v^2$.

*Air pressure on curved surfaces as determined
by measurements made in a wind, but disregarding
the additional lifting effect of wind.*

Camber $^1/_{12}$ width.

Work without forward flight.

Lilienthal's Bird-flight.

Fig. 2.

*Economy
in work during forward
flight in still air with
curved wings determined
from measurements
made in a wind.*

0,82 A − 6°
0,10 A − 3°
0,09 A   0°
0,09 "   3°
0,11 "   6°
0,15 "   12°
0,18 "   15°
0,29 "   20°
0,40 "   25°
0,60 "   30°
0,90 "   35°
0, "   60 "

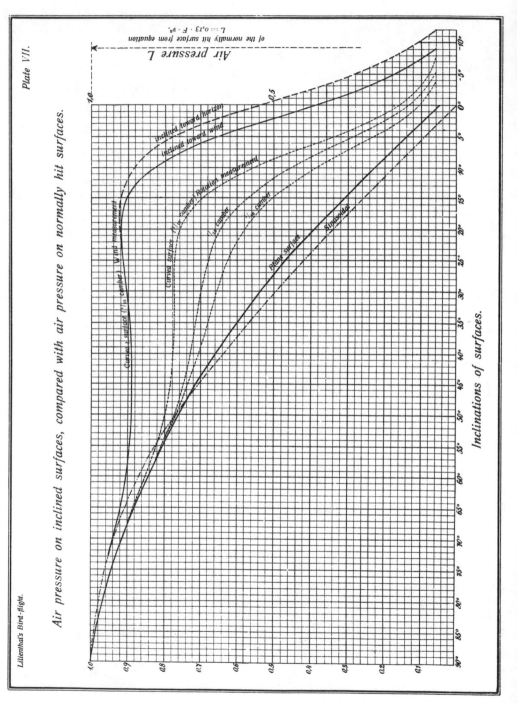

Lilienthal's Bird-flight.

Plate VII.

Air pressure on inclined surfaces, compared with air pressure on normally hit surfaces.

Inclinations of surfaces.

Air pressure L
of the normally hit surface from equation
L = 0,13 · F · v².

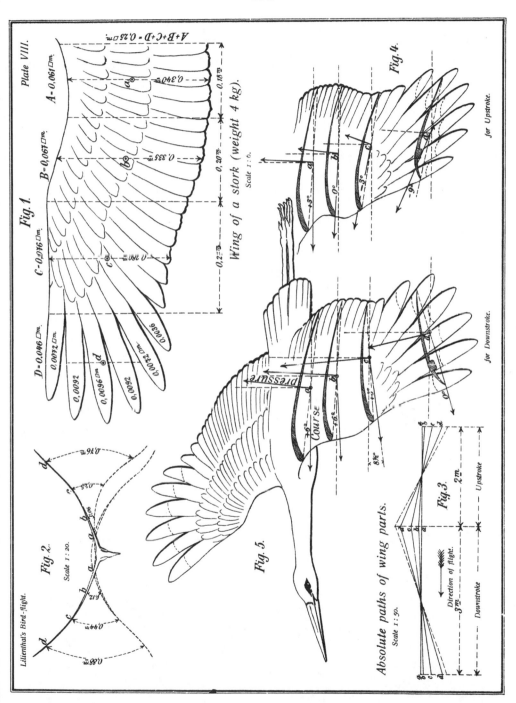

Plate VIII.

Fig. 1.

$A = 0.061 \,\square^m.$
$B = 0.067 \,\square^m.$
$C = 0.046 \,\square^m.$
$D = 0.046 \,\square^m.$

$A + B + C + D = 0.25 \,\square^m.$

Wing of a stork (weight 4 kg).
Scale 1 : 6.

Fig. 4.

for Upstroke.

for Downstroke.

Fig. 5.

Pressure

Course

Fig. 2.
Scale 1 : 20.

Lilienthal's Bird-flight.

Fig. 3.

Absolute paths of wing parts.
Scale 1 : 50.

Direction of flight.

Downstroke

Upstroke